THE WATER GARDEN

GARDEN

FRANCES PERRY
MBE VMH

 VAN NOSTRAND REINHOLD COMPANY
NEW YORK CINCINNATI TORONTO LONDON MELBOURNE

Library of Congress Catalog Card Number 81–2373
ISBN 0–442–28259–1

Printed in Hong Kong by
Everbest Printing Co., Ltd.

Published by
Van Nostrand Reinhold Company
A division of Litton Educational
Publishing, Inc. 135 West 50th Street,
New York, NY 10020, U.S.A.

Van Nostrand Reinhold Limited
1410 Birchmount Road,
Scarborough, Ontario M1P 2E7, Canada

First published in 1981 by Ward Lock Limited,
London, a Pentos Company

16 15 14 13 12 11 10 9 8 7 6 5 4 3 2 1

**Library of Congress Cataloging in Publication
Data**

Perry, Frances
  The water garden

  Includes indexes.
  1. Water gardens.   I. Title.
SB423.P39   635.9′674   81–2373
ISBN 0–442–28259–1   AACR2

Contents

Preface

Many years ago when I wrote my first book on water gardening there was only moderate interest in the subject. Understandably. Pool making was laborious, entailing not only soil excavation but the messy, heavy task of concrete mixing and then 'maturing' the concrete of the finished pool before plants could be installed.

Today life is much simpler. Thanks to modern techniques and materials the gardener can have a small pool installed *and planted* in a matter of hours. Plastic water lily baskets do not rot and are more readily retrieved for replanting purposes than the old cane kinds which were all we had prior to World War II. We can now go on to such refinements as waterfalls, fountains and even install biological control units to ensure perennially clear water if desired.

Tropical pools are becoming popular with those who have sun lounges and the like, while fish-keeping in aquaria is a popular pastime for millions. Plants are basic to success with all of these and today there are many types from which to choose.

For this new book, which incidentally, is not merely a revision of my earlier *Water Gardening*, I have had help and advice from many sources. They include my nephews David Everett of Anglo-Aquarium who has helped with plants for illustrations and details of equipment and Michael Everett of Wildwoods Water Garden Centre for much helpful advice; Denis Ingram and Andrew Shoolbred of Ward Lock on matters of presentation; Leslie Greenwood for his charming drawings; Florapic who provided many of the colour illustrations and my daughter-in-law Shirley Perry who typed all the manuscript.

Lastly I should like to thank my husband Roy Hay, not only for much helpful advice but for his never failing encouragement when the going got tough.

Enfield 1981   F. P.

1

The beginnings

Man has always interpreted water as an essential life-giving force. From earliest times dwellings have been erected in its vicinity, for without it there can be no crops, no flowers, no shade and no livestock. But, aside from such domestic uses, even primitive peoples probably appreciated the aesthetic qualities of water—the beauty of water plants, the movement of fish and the music made by a rushing stream or tumbling waterfall.

It accordingly seems reasonable to suppose that water features were an integral part of early gardens, including the legendary Hanging Gardens of Babylon. We know that Queen Hapshetset of Egypt (d.1480 BC) grew lotus and papyrus at Luxor and that water lily flowers were commonly placed on the mummies of High Priests during the XIX to XXI dynasties (dating from 2000 BC). A wreath of blue water lilies found in the tomb of Rameses II has been identified by botanists as *Nymphaea caerulea*, an African species still grown in gardens and still found wild in parts of the African continent.

The veneration in which water lilies were held is easily understood. Men of all races and times share certain basic aspirations. They look for immortality and they respect purity. Both of these are symbolized by water lily flowers, which with each spring and the returning waters, arise afresh—perfect and undefiled—from the mud and ugliness of summer baked ponds. This symbolism has led to the embodiment of water plants in many well known emblems. Thus, the furled sepals are believed to have suggested the basic design for the Ionic capital, which in turn led to the Greek fret or meander. This doubled again became the swastika, one of the oldest known written symbols, which, according to the arrangement of the links, represents good or evil, light or darkness, life or death, peace or conflict. The cornucopia—ancient symbol of fertility—is thought to have been suggested by the well-filled seedpods of water lilies and even the triangular effect assumed by the calyces of some species has been likened (like the shamrock) to a symbolic Trinity.

Added to these spiritual attributes are the more utilitarian ones that the seeds and tubers are edible and have been used as food by various races, that various medicinal remedies are claimed for certain species and that the tuberous root-stocks of the European *Nymphaea alba* were once used for dyeing a dark brown colour; and it is easy to appreciate the interest water lilies had for early man.

Water in gardens

All the world's great gardens have water features. Birds and butterflies, a rippling stream, cascading waterfall or spurting fountain bring movement and music to a garden. A flat stretch of water on the other hand reflects the moods of the weather. Sparkling sunshine, dancing raindrops or the gloom of storm clouds are all mirrored on its surface, as are nearby trees and pondside aquatics.

The simplicity of water is displayed to perfection in some of the great British gardens, particularly those laid out by such famous landscape architects as William Kent (1685–1748), Lancelot (Capability) Brown (1716–1783) and Humphrey Repton (1752–1818).

Calmness prevails in the placid lakes and series of canals featured at Studley Royal and Fountains Abbey in Yorkshire; also at Stourhead in Wiltshire where strategically placed grottos and temples accentuate pools and specimen trees. Sheffield Park Gardens in Sussex are built around a descending chain of five lakes, speckled with water lilies, while both formal and informal water features are to be found at Bodnant in Wales and Blenheim in Oxfordshire. But perhaps the most striking spectacle is the great cascade built by Joseph Paxton at Chatsworth in Derbyshire, where on still days a column of water more than 75 m (250 ft) high rises from a flat man-built canal.

France has always favoured elaborate fountain jets and water allées; among the most famous those designed by Le Nôtre at Versailles and Vaux-le-Vicomte. Evidence of the important part water played in the Renaissance Gardens of Italy can still be seen at the Villa d'Este at Tivoli.

The Bouchart Gardens on Vancouver Island, Canada, use water jets of elaborate patterns, which continually change shape and are illuminated at night in various colours. The water gardens at Longwood, Kennett Square, Pa. in the U.S.A. are very intricate and make skilful use of water plants as do those at Calloway Gardens in Georgia, while at Longue Vue in New Orleans jets of water play across a canal and there is a wall waterfall. These ideas have been inspired by the Generalife's Court of the Canal, designed centuries ago by Moorish gardeners. According to the Koran, Muhammed decreed that water should be kept in motion, dictates followed not only by the Moors and Persians but by Muslims generally. Ingenious schemes were devised for moving water from one part of the garden to another.

There are countless other water gardens like those of the Taj Mahal in India, the Shalimar Gardens of Kashmir, and the huge fountain jet War Memorial at Canberra in Australia which shoots up 1000 kg (3 tons) of water at 200 km (125 miles) per hour.

Waterfalls and cascades are an indispensable feature of Japanese gardens and there are innumerable small courtyard gardens, with pools and fountains, in Spain, North Africa and South America.

Water gardening today

For many years only those who possessed a natural lake or pond were able to grow aquatics, although baths, cisterns, sawn-down casks and other watertight receptacles were occasionally used to house the odd lily or a few goldfish.

Apart from these, water gardening attracted little interest until concrete became generally available in the 20th century. In 1848 *The Gardener's Chronicle*, answering a reader's query concerning the common white water lily *Nymphaea alba*, remarked that 'the roots of these things may sometimes be had in the nurseries, but are not usually kept'. In 1883 William Robinson, the great Victorian gardener, deplored the fact that 'unclean and ugly ponds deface our gardens; some have a mania for artificial water, the effect of water pleasing them so well that they bring it near their houses where they cannot have any of its good effects. But they have instead the filth that gathers in stagnant water and its evil smell on many a lawn'. Even in 1907 that great exponent of rock gardening, Reginald Farrer, was moved to counsel those about to make a water garden— 'Don't!'

Three things have changed these opinions—concrete, the late M. Latour Marliac, whose work with water lilies (see p. 29) did so much to popularise these plants, and biological research. Progressive studies by botanists and scientists revealed the interdependence of plant and animal life and how delicate was the balance between the two. Too much of one, wrong compost or even adulterated water produces discolouration and the 'evil smell' noted by Robinson. These findings paved the way to correct planting and consequently clear water.

The use of concrete meant that any gardener could have a pool if he so desired, and hundreds appeared in the early years of this century; and then after World War II new materials and new techniques were developed. These were easier for the amateur to handle and now thousands of new water gardens are constructed annually—not only in Britain and many European countries but in North and South America, Australia and New Zealand, Africa and the Orient.

They can be formal or informal, large or small, sunk to ground level or raised above the ground with a stone or brick coping; teamed with a rock garden or surrounded by a bog area containing moisture-loving plants, or used as a focal point in an open area of lawn or similar key situation. The permutations are endless, but to be successful the pool part particularly must be carefully sited and properly constructed, as described in the next chapter.

2

Pool construction

Few bog plants and virtually no aquatics flower well in shade. So, although a modicum of shade for part of the day is permissible in tropical countries, pools built in temperate or cold climates must be sited in an open position and exposed to full sun.

Overhanging trees are also undesirable as their fallen leaves create problems, although a belt of shrubs, a hedge or a building towards the north (or south in the southern hemisphere) will protect the pool from cold spring winds and so induce earlier flowering. A piped water supply (e.g. a tap) near at hand makes the filling and topping up of pools easy, also electricity and a recirculating water system if waterfalls or fountains are to be installed. These use the same water over and over again but need power in order to function.

All water gardens should be designed so as to fit in with their immediate surrounds. On a formal site, say the centre of a lawn or paved area surrounded by straight flower borders or hedges, the shape should be regular with the pool edges well defined. Squares, rectangles or circles are all permissible in such situations, also fountains, figures or stone artifacts to break the flatness. Planting however should be kept low to avoid fussiness, so water lilies, submerged oxygenators and perhaps a few variegated rushes or irises at the corners or near a fountain at the centre are all the plants required.

In informal situations the pool should be sunk into the ground so as to disguise its artificiality and have a few rocks—or a rock garden with a waterfall—perhaps a belt of shrubs or some bog plants towards the back or around its edges in order to give it a more natural appearance.

Shape and size

When the type of pool has been decided, consideration should be given to its shape and size. If the area is staked out with pegs and white tape before any soil is excavated it gives a rough idea of the ultimate effect.

Depth

Not every aquatic needs the same depth of water. Hardy water lilies, oxygenators and of course fish need from 30–90 cm (1–3 ft) according to climate and the vigour of the lilies; marginal aquatics require 5–10 cm (2–4 in) above their crowns, whereas bog plants do best in soil which is constantly damp but never waterlogged for any length of time. Tropical water lilies, which are widely grown in the United States and the warmer parts of Australia, do best with about 20 cm (8 in) of water above their crowns.

Types of pool

PUDDLED CLAY

This is an old-fashioned method, messy and difficult to make but still constructed occasionally by craftsmen in country areas. Primarily intended for cattle, some of those surviving near old farmhouses have changed their function through the years and been put to ornamental use.

Clay with straw or heather roots are puddled and pressed together—often by the plodding feet of carthorses—inside a pre-excavated hole. When properly made and filled with water, such a pool lasts for years.

CONCRETE POOLS

Concrete pools are strong and durable and may be fashioned to any shape, size and depth. They are still built in areas where vandalism or damage may occur—for example in public parks—also for formal pools constructed with broad or raised edges. Being extremely permanent however they are difficult to get rid of should changes in the garden be required and they also work out more expensive than flexible liners. Other drawbacks are a tendency for them to leak as they age, particularly following a severe winter when the expansion caused by a thick layer of ice results in stress. One way of absorbing this pressure is to float a large rubber ball or several logs of wood in the pool, then when a thick layer of ice forms release these objects by pouring boiling water over them, siphon out about 2.5–5 cm (1–2 in) of water and cover the holes with hessian. Directly a thaw sets in fill the pool again. Low energy consumption pond heaters will also keep a small water surface free of ice thus enabling fish to receive a supply of oxygen. In very cold areas however some people prefer to empty their pools in autumn, transferring the fish and plants to tubs or bowls under cover for the winter months.

Fresh concrete also releases free lime into the water, so before the pool is planted it must either be filled with water for several months before planting, then emptied and scrubbed, or the whole of the interior must be painted over with a neutralising and water-proofing agent. The latter can be bought from specialist aquatic dealers.

Start by excavating the deep part of the pool—intended for fish, lilies and the like—to the required size and depth plus 30 cm (12 in). Spread a 10 cm (4 in) layer of hardcore (stones, gravel, etc) over this, firm, and then add 2.5—5 cm (1–2 in) of sifted ashes or sand. Next spread 15 cm (6 in) of concrete over the whole of the base, inserting galvanised wire netting (5 cm (2 in) size or larger) half way through this operation, leaving good laps at the edges to turn up at the sides. Finally, smooth the base but before leaving the site score the edges to a width of 15 cm (6 in) so as to provide a rough key for the new concrete to adhere to when the sides are made. This should be applied (again 12.5–15 cm (5–6 in) thick) between a foundation made of oil-coated boards built in the form of a roofless, bottomless box. Make this box 15 cm (6 in) smaller than the base and stand it on the floor of the pool. Work the concrete round and round the spaces between the boards and the earth, solidifying it as work proceeds by tapping the boards with a hammer. After several days when it has hardened the box can be removed. It is also possible to build brick sides and foundations, covering these with 10–12.5 cm (4–5 in) of concrete.

Deep water pools are easier to construct and more likely to prove watertight if made to a conventional shape—square, rectangular or circular, but from then onwards the ultimate design or outline may be either formal or informal. With formal water gardens lay paving stones all round the sides and slightly overlapping the pool edge, or to make a pool with raised edges construct a coping of bricks and cover these with stone slabs or concrete up to the required height.

With an informal pool a shallow marginal surround should be constructed around the deep part. This can be quite shallow and fashioned to any shape and width. Normally a depth of 25–30 cm (10–12 in) allows for 10 cm (4 in) of concrete, 10–15 cm (4–6 in) of soil and 5–7.5 cm (2–3 in) of water. Leave the rim of the deep part 2.5 cm (1 in) lower than that of the surround so that when the pool is full of water it takes on the shape of these outer contours.

PREFABRICATED POOLS

Prefabricated pools are made of durable plastic reinforced with fibreglass mesh and come in various shapes—for example round, square or kidney-shaped. These are the easiest pools to install for it is only necessary to excavate a hole large enough to fit the shell, set it in place, test for levels with a spirit level, plant the aquatics and fill it with water. Some kinds have punched-out holes or built-in pockets to accommodate various types of aquatics at different planting levels. The drawbacks of these, however, are a sameness in design and their restricted size, for they are invariably made rather small to facilitate handling. They are also rather expensive.

FLEXIBLE POOL LINERS

Cheaper and almost as easy to install are pools made with flexible liners of butyl rubber or polyvinyl chloride, called PVC. A PVC liner woven with nylon has

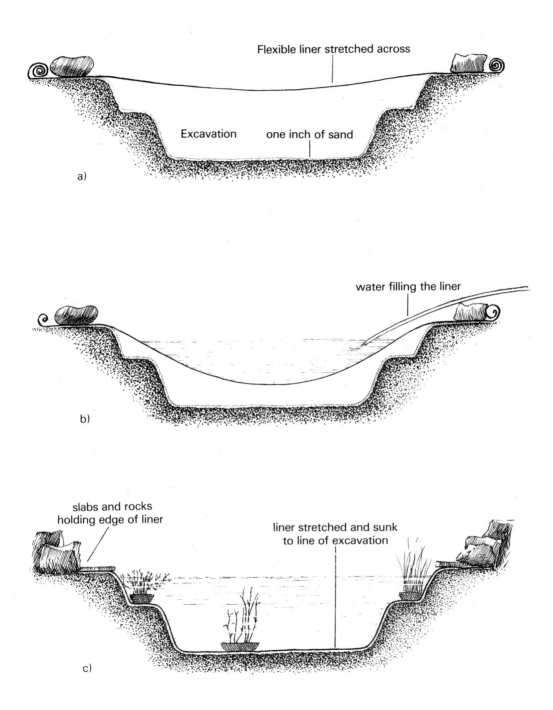

a) Flexible liner stretched across

Excavation   one inch of sand

b) water filling the liner

c) slabs and rocks holding edge of liner

liner stretched and sunk to line of excavation

Making a pool using a flexible liner. For extended description, please see text on next page.

exceptional strength for its flimsy appearance, being elastic enough to tolerate and stretch to fit uneven bottoms, and also withstand the pressure of ice and frost. Moreover, unlike the earliest rubber and plastic materials used for pond liners, modern types can be repaired with a special kit if accidentally punctured with a fork or a sharp instrument. PVC liners come in various colours but a dark shade is best as the base of the pool always turns black in time.

Start by excavating the soil to the required size, shape and depth—or series of depths. Line it with an inch of sand and then buy enough lining material to fit the pool's surface dimensions plus twice its maximum depth. Stretch the material across the top of the pool and weight it at the edges with bricks or rocks. Now run in the water and as the weight builds up the liner will stretch and sink to line the excavation. Now trim off any excess material apart from about 15 cm (6 in) all round the sides of the pool. Tuck this surplus under soil, or hide it beneath rocks or turf, plant the water lilies and aquatics in pots or baskets and set them in place.

Flexible liners can also be used to hold water in above-ground ponds, for example to carry streams or rock-pools designed to hold water for spilling over as waterfalls or ponds in a sunroom or garden lounge intended for tropical aquatics. The foundations supporting the latter must be strong and sturdy enough to take the weight of water and are usually made of bricks, heavy timber or concrete blocks.

SMALL RECEPTACLES FOR POOLS

Any vessel capable of holding water is a potential water garden. Baths, tanks and cattle troughs can be sunk into the ground, planted with aquatics and occasionally flooded over to keep the ground around damp enough to grow bog plants.

Wooden tubs and barrels previously used for beer, wine or vinegar make excellent small pools. They should be sawn in half so that the ultimate height is approximately 50 cm (20 in) and then thoroughly scrubbed inside and rinsed. If the staves are loose, pack them with clay and then fill the tub with water. As the wood swells it will gradually become watertight.

Now empty it again and put 15 cm (6 in) of compost (see p. 22) over the base, plant a small water lily and one or two aquatics in this and fill again with water. Tub gardens can either be sunk into the ground or used as they are, standing on a hard surface. Two or three fish should be placed in each to keep down mosquito larvae.

Tubs which have held oil, tar, wood preservatives or other oily substances are not suitable for miniature pools. They are almost impossible to clean properly unless burnt over inside, and neither fish nor plants will thrive in tainted containers.

3

Water garden features
and accessories

Moving water

Anyone who makes a water garden often wonders if movement should be introduced, possibly by constructing a waterfall, building a stream or installing a fountain. The agitation produced by any of these has both advantages and disadvantages. On the credit side is the fact that water in motion is aesthetically pleasing, soothing to the eye and musical to the ear. The splash created by falling water raises the oxygen level which benefits the fish, while its constant movement prevents dust and debris settling as surface scum and inhibits the growth of fine algae like those found in green water. Against this is the undeniable fact that falling water lowers the pool's temperature, which is fine on a hot summer day but is not so good in cold weather. Also water lilies (particularly) will not flower well if they are continually doused with spray; the blooms just close and sink.

However, if the fountain or waterfall is sited away from aquatic plantings, is used with discretion on cold days and draws its water supply from the pool itself these difficulties may be overcome. The best answer is to recirculate the water by means of an electrically operated pump, which will use and re-use the same water over and over again but can be turned off when required.

Pumps

There are two kinds of pool pumps—surface and submersible. The latter is the easier to install and usually the cheaper to purchase. It operates entirely under water with the whole assembly—base, motor, pump and fountain head—contained in a single unit. It works soundlessly and should be submerged in the pool to enable the pump chamber, which contains a centrifugal impeller, to keep taking in water through a strainer and driving it upwards. This it does either through a jet attached to the pump in the case of a fountain, or through a connecting tube between the pump and the highest point from which the water will flow if you are making a waterfall.

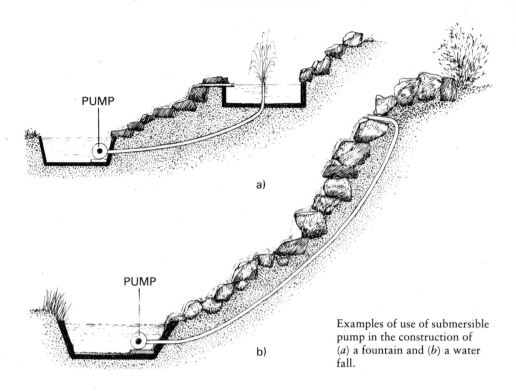

a)

b)

Examples of use of submersible pump in the construction of (*a*) a fountain and (*b*) a water fall.

Cheaper submersible pumps are usually adequate for small to medium pools which have only one fountain jet or one waterfall, whereas the larger pumps are capable of operating high volume water features. According to make and water pressure these are capable of producing an output of 1000–15 000 litres (220–3300 gal) per hour, with (in the case of a fountain) a head of water approximately 1 m (3 ft) high.

If more height is required the output is naturally reduced because of the extra push needed to drive the water. However, aquatic specialists and pump manufacturers will advise on the output potential of any model and relate this to your own requirements. Naturally the more water which gets through in a given time, the stronger the flow from the waterfall or fountain. All submersible pumps should be fitted with a length of waterproof cable sealed into the unit and long enough to reach an electricity point which is suitably protected and has a weather-proof connector. This part should be undertaken by a qualified electrician— water and electricity are not good team-mates! However, a number of low voltage pumps are also available, operated through a transformer (away from the water); these are mandatory in some countries.

Surface pumps are more difficult and expensive to install although they have greater potential, especially for large pools or where a series of fountains or cascades and waterfalls are required. Some models are capable of an output of 30 000 litres (6600 gal) or more per hour.

Surface pumps must be kept outside the pool in a ventilated but waterproof house, preferably one built of brick or paving stones and of a size sufficient to accommodate the valves which control the flow of water as well as the pump. A drainage hole should be built into the floor and connected to a sump or drain. This is necessary in order to prevent flooding. Another requirement is a removable cover capable of keeping out rain, but not so tightly sealed as to induce condensation—which could damage the pump.

Surface pumps are inevitably a little noisy and of course entail more plumbing than the submerged kinds. They must not be set too high above the level of the water or the suction lift will not operate successfully. Normally, there is a suction lift margin of just over 1 m (3 ft) with most models but do check on this with your dealer before building the pump house. The intake pipe from the pool will have a strainer and foot valve to prevent a flow back of water when the pump is idle, and the outlet pipe will naturally be taken to the highest point where water is required so that it can find its way downwards when the pump is working.

To start the flow the pump must first be primed so the suction pipe needs to be filled with water—this is most conveniently done with a hose after first fitting the foot valve. When the pipe is full start the pump. It should then continue to function until the pump is turned off. Alternatively, a priming tank can be fitted. In some makes this is built into the pump.

Waterfalls, cascades and streams

These are usually constructed in conjunction with informal or natural water gardens. There are exceptions—like the water staircase at Chatsworth in Derbyshire—which is patently artificial but impressive on account of its magnitude and skilful design, but normally in a formal or semi-formal setting fountains, either wall types or free-standing, are the most appropriate.

Waterfalls look best when they are built into a rock garden and so arranged that a flow of water from high up drops in one or a series of cascades to a pool at the lowest level. However, when building such features it must be remembered that in nature water never flows in a straight line. There may be one straight drop but then the water makes its way down through the softest rocks, avoiding obstacles, to finish up finally at the lowest point. The same principle applies to streams, which should gently meander in soft curves. Always start a waterfall high up but not right at the top of the rock garden if you want it to look natural.

Streams and small cascades can be constructed on site using concrete but, as with concrete pools, once made they cannot easily be removed. It is also hard work building them and unless the base is firm and solid, often difficult on a sloping rock garden; they may leak around the edges since concrete does not bond effectively with natural stone.

However, a satisfactory method of constructing waterfalls or streams, using natural stone or concrete, is by first excavating the area to the required depth and width, then lining it with a flexible liner and finally constructing the water features *over* this waterproof membrane. Should leaks then occur no water will be lost, but will ultimately return to the pool to be recirculated. If you do not wish to go to this trouble, again your dealer can help. Most aquatic specialists sell fibreglass basins and troughs for waterfall basins. I prefer those with lips (sometimes called dripstones) since these have an overhang, providing a sounding box behind. Then when the dripping water falls from one trough to the next it makes a pleasant musical sound which is delightfully refreshing on a hot summer day.

Unfortunately fibreglass shells do not mellow or look as natural as concrete, so if you can call on labour to help lift them, another alternative is to build concrete shells by digging out shallow moulds in a spare corner of ground (they need not be all the same size) and lining these with polythene. Make a stiff concrete mix using one part cement by volume to two of coarse builders' sand and three of aggregate, the latter composed of washed gravel or stones varying in size from 5–20 mm ($\frac{1}{4}$–$\frac{3}{4}$ in). Avoid adding anything of an organic nature or in time the concrete could leak. Pour the mixture into the mould to a depth of about 10 cm (4 in), bending and embedding some galvanised chicken wire netting half-way through before smoothing it to the required shape. Leave a lip at the front of each shell, a little lower down than the rest of the edges, so that when water builds up inside it will pour out without overflowing from the sides. If the shells can be made away from the site and then lifted and bedded into position, it will be easier to angle them to give the best flow of water—easily tested with a can of water.

Support the shells, fill all spaces around them with pieces of rock, and put soil and plants close to the edges. If you have made the shells with a high enough rim and can control the flow of water, there should be little or no leakage. The normal spray from splashing water will benefit nearby plants.

A water course allowing water to run through rocks to a pool can be built in the same way, either in conjunction with or instead of a waterfall. Simulated streams made of fibreglass can be obtained in prefabricated sections which when joined will also convey water. Alternatively, the soil can be excavated to a depth of about 30 cm (12 in) and the cavity lined with about 10 cm (4 in) of concrete. Embed a few rocks here and there to give the stream a more natural appearance. It is important however to see that the sides are high enough to retain the water without flooding; use a cheap liner beneath the concrete to be certain of a waterproof stream.

Fountains and spouting ornaments

Aquatic dealers stock various types of fountains, from large models capable of throwing jets of water many feet in the air to smaller but sophisticated models suitable for garden pools.

A colourful planting of waterside plants blending happily with the rest of the garden.

A long, narrow canal-type pool backed by delphiniums and other herbaceous plants; white arum lilies, sagittarias and irises in the foreground.

Most of them consist of a single central plume which may be surrounded by a number of jets—straight, fan-shaped, bell-like or cascading—capable of providing a wide range of spray patterns.

There is also a wide range of spouting ornaments available, in stone or plastic, consisting of dolphins, seals, frogs and other animals or human figures. Particularly popular are lion's heads which can be mounted on a wall above a pool. Water, of course, is supplied to these ornaments by a small pump such as those used to supply water to fountains or cascades.

Lighting the water garden

In recent years modern equipment has greatly enhanced the pleasure derived from water gardens by illuminating pools, cascades and fountains—as well as their surrounding plants. These can be lit from below or above. Waterproof electric lamps are available that may be floated on the water or weighted so that they are just below the surface or even rest on the bottom of the pool. Alternatively if they are mounted on spikes these may be pushed into the ground and adjusted to any angle to illuminate poolside plants or trees and shrubs in the water garden area.

Lamps are available in various colours and while one may derive a certain amount of fun blending various colours, my own preference is for ordinary clear lamps. There is something to be said, however, for red lamps at certain times as these accentuate and enhance the colour of any trees or shrubs with reddish foliage (such as *Cotinus coggygria*) growing near the pool.

Lighting equipment comes in a variety of types and sizes with wall brackets for permanent fixtures as well as the soil spikes already mentioned. Particularly interesting are the sets of low voltage lamps, supplied complete with transformer and a number of lamps, which may be quickly moved from one position to another. Thus when an attractive group of, say, primulas are in flower, this may be singled out and illuminated and then when the flowers are over, the lamps can be moved to spotlight some astilbes or other later blooming plants. Because they operate on low voltage this can be managed quite quickly and safely.

But perhaps lighting is most attractive when it is used to illuminate fountains. Lighting catching the iridescent sheen of the trembling droplets brings magic to a garden at night and thus greatly adds to the overall enjoyment of the water feature.

Especially attractive is the lighting of fountains that produce an automatic change sequence of patterns. In the world renowned Bouchart Gardens on Vancouver Island, British Columbia, there are superb fountains which give constant changes of spray patterns and changes of lighting as well. We cannot be quite as ambitious in small gardens of course, but in a limited fashion we can create some of these effects.

Indoor pools

With the present general tendency towards smaller gardens, particularly in urban areas, many people have to fit their gardening activities into limited space. In recent years garden rooms built on to houses have become popular for growing plants in as well as for providing extra living space for the family.

Since these are nearly always built on a hard surface, usually concrete, and are normally within reach of essential services, small indoor pools can easily be installed in them. The pool may be of a temporary nature, fashioned from a prefabricated shell supported at the sides with stout timber or else built of concrete with strong raised sides, ideally with a plug connected to a drain. It could also be set into the ground as an ornamental feature, finished off with a broad stone, brick or even marble surround.

The advantages of an indoor pool are several. When the children are young it can be filled with sand and used as a sandpit, or if soil-warming cables are laid over the base and covered with 5 cm (2 in) of sand, it can be used to house tender garden plants in winter. When a garden frame-light is popped over the top the pool can then do duty as a propagator, or when used for water plants which have died down in winter, boards can be laid over the top to provide a temporary table for games or other activities.

If it is converted to a permanent pool with year round interest, unusual plants can be grown in the corners such as *Cyperus papyrus*, the Egyptian paper plant, or *Thalia dealbata*, a noble foliaged plant with heads of drooping reddish flowers. In the deep part of the pool tropical blue water lilies and the golden water poppy, *Hydrocleys nymphoides*, provide shade and colour; exotic types of fish can be installed and at the edges plants like the parrot's feather, *Myriophyllum proserpinacoides*, will trail over the sides like green curtains.

Different depths can be obtained by building brick pockets in the pool, and filling them with soil so as to take shallow water aquatics. The deepest part should normally be around 30 cm (12 in). Soil mixes and methods of planting are identical with those described in Chapter 4.

In an indoor pool the fragrant night blooming water lilies have more appeal, particularly when a spot light or underwater lighting reveals the extent of their beauty. There is no general pattern for indoor pools except that plenty of light, including top lighting, is essential. I built one once in a central position with 75 cm ($2\frac{1}{2}$ ft) raised concrete sides, but I have seen another let into the floor in a corner position, the broad ledges at the back used to hold pots of large house plants which gave the pool character even in winter. A small heater (p. 21) will keep the water from getting too cold so that the fish remain active all winter.

It is also possible to install a small wall fountain and submersible pump if the pool is large enough and you like the sound of running water. There are neat little fountains of around 30 cm (12 in) in diameter which are designed for indoor use even when there is not enough room for a large pond. In fact there are all sorts of permutations on the idea of indoor pool shape and design, and what you can grow. A visit to the—admittedly larger—pools in the greenhouses at Kew or Edinburgh, or indeed any of the world's botanic gardens, will give you an idea of the variety of plants it is possible to grow.

Heating the pool

Electric pool heaters are so simple to install that they only need to be placed on the surface of an indoor pool, where the block of expanded polystyrene in which they are suspended keeps them afloat. In the case of outdoor pools containing fish it is also well worth while installing one or more of these heaters, because they will keep a small area free of ice in winter, thus enabling the fish to obtain oxygen. Heaters are particularly useful in very shallow pools, such as those built in rock gardens where the ice could freeze solid in a prolonged cold spell.

One heater will take care of around 2.8 sq m (30 sq ft) of surface water in Britain, rather less in colder climates.

Fish feeders

After a while one learns how much food to give fish at any one time—normally all they can consume in five minutes. Never give them so much that it drops to the floor of the pool, to rot and cause contamination.

An easy method of giving them all they want without waste is to use one of the fish food feeders obtainable from dealers. These automatically dispense food when activated by the fish. The latter come to the surface to feed so one can enjoy the sight of them tucking into their favourite food because the same feeder is able to dispense various types of food for many kinds, types and sizes of fish.

Herons

In some areas herons can cause many losses among ornamental fish. The heron does not fly into the pool. It lands alongside and walks into the water. Complete protection is obtained if a square mesh plastic net is suspended just below the surface of the water. The heron tries to walk into the pool, is discouraged by the net and goes elsewhere.

These birds are reputed to be great respecters of other herons' territory and placing life-size, plastic models of herons near or in a pool is often successful in keeping visiting herons away. (See also p. 166).

4

Planting and cultivation

Time to plant

Most water plants, whether they go in deep water, pond margins or bog gardens, are best transplanted in spring and early summer, before vegetative growth is far enough advanced for them to receive much of a check. The lengthening hours of daylight and increasing warmth will then encourage quick root development so that they soon become established.

Completely submerged aquatics which possess few if any roots, on the other hand, can be moved at any time during the growing season. The same remark applies to floating plants.

Planting water lilies

Although hardy water lilies can be planted directly into the soil spread over the bottom of a pool, the most satisfactory method is to grow them in baskets since these can be quickly and easily recovered for division or replanting. Aquatic baskets made of sturdy plastic with apertures round the sides (to allow root egress) are obtainable from specialist growers. These should be lined with thin plastic sheeting to retain the soil in the early stages.

Hardy water lilies have two sorts of tubers: one kind has thick central rootstocks with roots emanating from their bases, like celery plants; the other has banana-shaped rhizomes growing horizontally like bearded irises. Young plants must be installed upright or horizontally according to whichever type they belong to, and planted in heavy loam reinforced with either one sixth of its bulk of well rotted cow-manure, or about $\frac{1}{4}$ litre (10 fl oz or half a pint) of coarse bonemeal per basket. If the loam is poor add also a handful of soluble dried blood or general fertilizer.

Plant very firmly, using soil on the damp side so that it packs well down and leave the crown of each plant just clear of the surface. Finally topdress the basket with 19 mm ($\frac{3}{4}$ in) of well washed, pea-sized shingle. This prevents fish from nuzzling the soil, exposing plant roots and making the water cloudy.

Except in tropical climates tender water lilies are usually started in heat 18–21°C (64–70°F) under glass. They have small rounded tubers which are sprouted in small pots of sandy soil, then transplanted without root disturbance into larger containers of a soil mixture as recommended for hardy lilies. In every instance it is essential not to put the freshly planted roots in too deep water. Raise the baskets on bricks at first so that the lily crowns are barely below the water surface. Only when new growth appears should they be lowered—and then by easy stages—to the floor of the pool.

Marginal aquatics, submerged oxygenators and floaters

Marginal aquatics are easier to manage than water lilies since only their roots need to be submerged. The depth of water above their crowns will vary according to the ultimate height of the plants, but by and large, 5–15 cm (2–6 in) is enough for most of the genera mentioned in this book. A few plants, like water forget-me-nots and kingcups (*Caltha* species), are very adaptable and will do equally well in wet soil or shallow water. The important thing is to keep the roots always damp or they may die.

Marginal aquatics may be planted either in pockets built into the sides of the pool during construction, or in pots or aquatic baskets of good loamy soil. No fertilizer is necessary for these plants since rich feeding tends to make them coarse and over rampant for small pools. It is also advisable to topdress the soil with clean shingle to prevent fish from disturbing it.

Submerged aquatics have scarcely any roots and once disturbed—as for replanting—will float to the surface unless anchored. A few, like water moss (*Fontinalis antipyretica*) and the stoneworts (*Chara* spp.), attach themselves naturally to stones which can then be dropped as they are into the pool, but most should be artificially weighted. The simplest way of doing this is by grouping several stems together, then gently clipping a narrow strip of lead round the base of each bunch before dropping them into the water.

Floating aquatics present no planting problems; it is only necessary to place them on the water surface and leave them alone.

Bog plants

Bog plants have varying needs. Some like alkaline soils but the majority prefer acid or neutral conditions. There are plants like *Primula rosea* which tolerate standing water for brief periods; *Iris kaempferi* will grow in shallow water during the growing season. Most bog plants require constant moisture in the vicinity of their roots. Generally speaking they require richer soil than aquatic plants, and damp ground rather than wet. The installation of piped water, with pop-up sprinklers or taps to which oscillating sprinklers can be attached, provides an easy method of applying water in dry weather. Plenty of organic matter in the soil retains moisture as well as soluble plant foods. Another idea is to excavate the bog area 22–30 cm (9–12 in) deep and line the base and 15 cm (6 in) up the sides with 500 gauge plastic sheeting. Place 5 cm (2 in) of stones in the base and then return the soil. A certain amount of water will then be retained by the plastic yet the top soil will be well drained.

When making a bog garden it is advisable to enrich the existing soil by working in plenty of organic material such as well rotted manure, garden compost, leaf soil or moist peat. Also add some coarse sand if the ground is heavy clay and 50 g/m² (2 oz/sq yd) of a balanced fertilizer containing nitrogen, potash and phosphate. In succeeding years mulch the ground between the plants with mushroom compost, leaf soil or rotted manure. Do this in spring after the plants have been divided (if necessary) or new plants have been installed.

Summer care

During the summer months, apart from controlling any pests which may attack water plants (see pp. 165–6), a certain amount of pruning will be necessary in order to keep them under control. Due to the fact that they are rarely short of moisture or nutriment, many aquatics grow extremely vigorously. This may not matter in large lakes but can be a nuisance in small pools. Similarly some plants like alismas, sparganiums and typhas produce a great deal of seed, so that the spent flowers must be regularly removed in order to prevent crops of unwanted seedlings.

Discoloured leaves and dead water lily flowers should be cut back as close to the crowns of the plants as possible. To get rid of leaves which have become detached, unwanted floating plants, scum and surface algae, hose the water vigorously and drive all the debris to one corner, then lift it out with a fishnet. Surface scum often occurs on freshly planted pools but is easily removed by drawing a sheet of newspaper across the top of the water. It adhers to the paper, leaving the water clear to reflect the sky and mirror pondside plants.

Occasionally underwater oxygenators grow too luxuriantly and choke other plants. Drag out the surplus with a garden rake and from time to time lift, divide and replant marginal aquatics.

Hardy water lilies in baskets can be kept in the same containers for four to five years if fed each summer with bonemeal 'pills'. These are made by moulding together bonemeal and wet clay into golf-ball size spheres and pushing one or more—according to the vigour of the plant—down into the soil. A word of warning—do wear gloves when handling bonemeal as a precaution against anthrax, which has been known to occur in unsterilized bonemeal from Asia.

The bog garden too will need weekly attention. Remove dead flowers, weed between plants, apply mulches early in the season and fill any gaps with temporary moisture-loving annuals like mimulus and impatiens to keep the borders bright with colour throughout the summer.

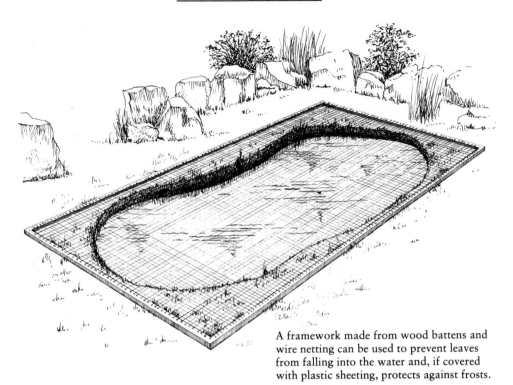

A framework made from wood battens and wire netting can be used to prevent leaves from falling into the water and, if covered with plastic sheeting, protects against frosts.

Autumn and winter in the water garden

In early autumn leaves start to fall from nearby trees and most of the aquatics will die down fouling the water with decaying vegetation. These leaves must either be trapped before they get into the pool or be dredged out regularly. A simple method of catching them is by building a light framework of timber laths and 2.5 cm (1 in) mesh wire netting. This should be slightly larger than the pool and when laid across the water will trap the leaves. This same framework has winter uses since it can be employed as a protection against frost. Covered with plastic sheeting or some hessian wraps (burlap) it will ward off quite heavy frosts, although anything which cuts out light must be removed after every thaw to prevent premature growth starting on the lilies.

Pine branches laid across small pools also afford protection, and another idea much practised in Britain is to float a log or large rubber ball in the pool as described on p. 9. The only drawback with this method is the need to top up the water again after every thaw.

In very cold climates with prolonged periods of freezing, concrete pools (in particular) may have to be emptied and the plants and fish taken inside for the winter.

Marginal aquatics and bog plants should be cut back when killed by frost, otherwise they provide winter sanctuary for hibernating pests. In the bog garden fork between plants, but only deep enough to stir the soil and remove perennial weeds. A few of the tender kinds may need winter protection so before frosts occur they should be taken into a frame or greenhouse.

Except in warm climates tropical water lilies *must* be over-wintered under cover in a frost free place. Cold soon affects the leaves, which then die off, after which the water lilies should be dug up and washed. It is almost impossible to keep the mother plants alive in winter but at the base of most will be found small walnut-sized tubers. Night blooming sorts often have small tubers on top of the old one as well as below. Remove all these tubers and store them in slightly moist sand in closed containers until spring. (See p. 30 for details of starting these and planting them out later.)

Keep all outside pools which contain plants and fish full of water in winter, and do not feed the fish between early winter (November in Britain) and early spring. They should then be given a rich protein diet to build them up again ready for the summer (see p. 171).

Replanting

Sooner or later it becomes necessary to empty and replant small pools. These only hold a restricted amount of water and soil, and when the latter becomes exhausted water lilies tend to bunch their leaves and thrust them out of the water, resulting in a loss of flowers. Marginal aquatics become weak or straggly.

Large expanses of water are less of a problem and can go for years with little attention from the gardener. However, when they silt up or become dirty and overgrown and cleaning out becomes necessary, it is best to call in a firm which specializes in this work. Dredging out mud and water from large lakes is heavy and dirty work, requiring special pumps and equipment.

To go back to small pools, few of these have outlets for emptying purposes, and it is of course quite impossible to fit plugs to plastic liners. A raised concrete pool in a formal situation may have built-in plugs or runaways connected to drainpipes running into a sump, drain or ditch. These are usually controlled by a stopcock, operated by a removable long-arm key; the whole enclosed in a small brick or stone chamber disguised by a moveable paving stone. Remember though that all runaways and plug holes are liable to become blocked with mud or plant roots unless the outlet from the pool is kept clear or covered with mesh. They are also expensive to install.

Alternatively, the water can be baled out by hand—a laborious business—or pumped out with an electrically powered pump of the submersible type, such as is used for working fountains (p. 7), but the simplest method is to siphon it out. All you need is a length of hose long enough to reach from the pool down to a drain or ditch. The latter must be at a lower level than that of the pool. Place one end of the hose in the pool and if possible connect the other end to a tap. Turn on the latter and when the flow of water has driven out any air in the hose disconnect the tap end and let the water siphon out backwards and run away.

If there is no tap available fill a length of hose with water and pinch the ends together to prevent air access. Place one end in the pool and release the pressure. The water should then run out but if it does not it may be necessary to remove the air by drawing it out with the mouth. A messy business—but it works! Whichever method is used it is advisable to run the water through a small hand-net in case fish are drawn into the pipe.

Once the pool is empty remove fish and plants. Keep the former in baths of clean water and cover the latter with wet hessian until you are ready to deal with them. Scrub the inside of the pool using a mild disinfectant, empty, rinse and refill with clean water.

Replant the lilies after washing them and cutting away all the old roots and pieces of tuber. Retain only the strongest young shoots with 7.5–15 cm (3–6 in) of attached tuber and plant as described on p. 22.

Aquatics and oxygenators, after being washed in a very mild solution of water and permanganate of potash crystals (enough to turn the liquid pale pink), should be replanted in fresh soil. Fish go in last.

5

Water lilies

The genus *Nymphaea* with 50 species of frost-hardy and tropical water lilies has a long and historical association with Man. The genus is widespread, most countries of the world having representatives, with the greater number in India and Africa. There they have probably been cultivated for thousands of years since according to Charles Pickering in *Chronological History of Plants* (1879) representations of *Nymphaea stellata* are 'distinctly figured in the cave-temples of Adjunta and various Braminical cave-temples elsewhere in India'.

The classical writers of early Greece and Rome became acquainted with water lilies through contact with Ancient Egypt. Herodotus for example (b.484 BC) wrote that when the Nile 'is full and has made the plains like a sea, great numbers of lilies, which the Egyptians call lotus, spring up in the water; these they gather and dry in the sun, then having pounded the middle of the lotus, which resembles a poppy, they make bread of it and bake it. The root also of this lotus is fit for food, and is tolerably sweet, and is round, and of the size of an apple'. H. S. Conard in *The Water Lilies* (1905) considers that this description refers to the white-flowered *N. lotus*. Diodorus Cronus (110 BC) also mentions the lotus of the Nile being used for bread and so does Dioscorides in his *Materia Medica* (2nd century AD). The latter describes 'the Egyptian lotus which grows in plains flooded by the water' (of the Nile) thus: 'The stem resembles that of Nelumbo, having a white flower like a lily which, they say, opens at sunrise, and closes at sunset, and the head is altogether hidden under water, and again emerges at sunrise. The head is like a very large poppy; in it is seed like millet, which the Egyptians dry and beat into bread. It has a root like a quince, which is also eaten both raw and cooked; when cooked it resembles the yolk of an egg.'

There are many more references from early writers regarding the virtues of water lilies not only for food but for religious purposes (see Chapter 1), also medicinally for dysentery and bowel complaints and as an aphrodisiac. In Australia *N. gigantea* is eaten (tubers, leaf stalks and fruit) by aborigines.

From an aesthetic angle the flowers are delightfully symmetrical and often highly fragrant, and they show a wide range of colour. They may be white, cream, yellow, pink, red, mauve, blue or bicoloured and of a size ranging from tiny blossoms which can slip through a wedding ring to flowers the size of tea-plates. They can be single, semi-double or double, floating on the water or raised on stems up to 30 cm (12 in) high. The young seedling leaves are pale green and almost transparent, the mature foliage dark green, often blotched with chocolate and with entire or crinkled edges.

Methods of growth and reproduction vary considerably in the species. For example, the European N. *alba* has thick tuberous rootstocks and increases from 'eyes' or side pieces, while both the North American N. *odorata* and N. *tuberosa* produce rhizomes with brittle nodules round their sides which break off to make new plants. Another species, N. *mexicana*, increases by throwing out runners after the fashion of a strawberry plant. Most tender nymphaeas however make black walnut-sized tubers which may not survive after flowering but as they die down in winter—or during periods of drought—they produce small tubers round the base of the old plant, or sometimes on top of it, and these grow on to make new stock. Finally a few species have viviparous leaves and produce new plantlets at the axil of leaf and leaf-stalk. When the water level falls these sink into the mud and the little plantlets root down to make new plants.

From these species a few dedicated hybridists have raised some outstanding cultivars. The first development came in 1850 with the appearance of a hybrid called *Nymphaea × devoniensis*. This was created by Joseph Paxton, gardener to the Duke of Devonshire (who was also the first European to flower *Victoria amazonica*), and it was succeeded by a whole spate of hybrids produced by the late Monsieur Marliac of France. Joseph Bory Latour-Marliac was born at Granges (Lot-et-Garonne) in 1830, and since his father and his great-uncle (Baron Bory de Saint Vincent) were eminent botanists it is to be presumed that he took an interest in plants from early childhood. Certainly he soon forsook his intended classical career after graduating, and due to the Revolution of 1848, left Paris and his studies to manage the family property in Garonne. After his marriage he settled at Temple-sur-Lot, and began to collect tropical plants, including a 6 hectare (15-acre) plot containing the most comprehensive collection of forest bamboos in the world.

In 1858 chance led him to an article by Professor G. Lévêque in *La Revue du Jardin des Plantes de Paris* concerning tropical water lilies. The writer praised their beauty and lamented the fact that such colours and shapes were not available in the hardy kinds known and grown in the ponds and rivers of France. At this time only the white N. *alba* was grown outside, but Marliac was so enthused by the idea of coloured water lilies that he began to collect and hypridize species from all over the world.

One very useful discovery was a carmine-red sport from N. *alba*. This originated in a lake at Neriko, Sweden, and pollen from its flowers helped to put 'pink' into N. *alba*, N. *tuberosa* and N. *odorata*. Other forms came from various countries including the yellow *N. mexicana* from Mexico, which gave Marliac his first hardy yellow water lily which he called 'Marliacea Chromatella' in 1881.

Between 1883 and 1890 plant followed plant—reds, pinks, dwarfs, giant-flowered and double forms. Those worthy of Marliac's special approbation received his patronymic—they became Marliacea something or other, or Laydekeri—after his son-in-law Maurice Laydeker. For trade reasons the details of his hybridizing methods were never divulged and they seem to have died with him. Few new good cultivars have appeared in recent years (he died in 1911) but thanks to his work the world is richer by some 70 hardy water lilies.

Most tropical day-blooming water lilies however we owe to the Missouri Botanic Garden in St Louis, where an English-born hybridist, the late George Pring, was as interested in these as Marliac was with the hardies. The first pure white cultivar 'Mrs George H. Pring' originated in these gardens and was followed by a host of blue, purple, pink, reddish and white forms, also, thanks to the discovery of an African yellow lily, *N. burttii*, plants with yellow, peach and rose flowers. Pring was also responsible for a number of night-blooming cultivars.

Hardy water lilies are best planted outside in spring or early summer, when the first young leaves appear, that is, between the end of March and early June in Britain. April/June, however, may be better in colder areas like parts of the United States and northern Europe. Hardy water lilies can be left outside all winter provided their roots are below the level of freezing, but in very cold climates the roots should be lifted and over-wintered in moist sand in a cool dark place; temperatures around 10°C (50°F).

Tender water lilies however should not be planted outside until the water is warm enough to encourage growth. Temperatures lower than 21°C (70°F) tend to induce dormancy from which the plants are slow to recover. In Britain this may be June or even July, dependent on the weather, which is why most people grow tropical water lilies in sun-warmed sunlounges or greenhouses. In southern Europe and the American midwest they can usually be planted outside by the middle of May; a little earlier in the south, but in the east and Great Lakes region the first week in June. Similarly in Australia, South Africa and parts of South America, September and October will be the most suitable months for planting outside, but in the tropics they can remain outside all the year round.

Hardy water lilies—a selection of species and cultivars

Robust varieties for large pools and lakes—marked 'A'.
Surface area covered: 0.5–0.75 sq m (5–8 sq ft).
Recommended depth of water: 60–90 cm (2–3 ft).

Medium growers for garden pools—marked 'B'.
Surface area covered: 0.35–0.65 sq m (4–7 sq ft).
Recommended depth of water: 60 cm (2 ft).

Very small lilies for tubs and rock pools—marked 'C'.
Recommended depth of water: 22.5–37.5 cm (9–15 in).

WHITE AND CREAM FLOWERS

Nymphaea alba (European white water lily; platter-dock) A hardy, robust species; crowded leaves to 30 cm (1 ft) across; flowers 10–12.5 cm (4–5 in) across, yellow stigmas. Cultivar 'Candidissima', larger flowered, with a long season until frost. A.

'Albatross' (Marliac 1910) Snow white with golden anthers; leaves purple when young developing to green at maturity. B.

N. candida is a pretty little species widely distributed throughout north and Arctic Europe and Asia, south to Bohemia and the Himalayas. The flowers are small, pure white, uniformity of colour being relieved by red stigmas; the foliage is green. C.

'Caroliniana Nivea' (Marliac 1893) Large white, fragrant flowers. C.

'Colossea' (Marliac 1901) Very large flowers with white to flesh coloured petals; free flowering, from spring until frosts; leaves green. A.

N. fennica is the Finnish water lily and is very rarely seen in cultivation, probably because it requires extremely cold water such as a pool fed with spring water. The flowers are pure white, small and cup-shaped, the bright green foliage also being well below average size. B.

'Gladstoniana' (Richardson U.S.) Magnificent cultivar with pure white flowers 15–20 cm (6–8 in) across, full of golden stamens; deep green leaves which are very strong and tend to rise out of the water. A.

'Gloire de Temple-sur-Lot' (Marliac 1913) The finest double water lily with up to 100 finely cut petal segments; blooms creamy-white but unfortunately not very prolific. A and B.

'Gonnêre', also known as 'Crystal White' (Marliac 1914). Snow white double flowers, the petals thicker textured than preceding, with prominent green sepals. The blooms sit squatly in the water; foliage green. A and B.

'Hermine' (Marliac 1910) Medium sized, star-shaped flowers, pure white, standing just above the water, free blooming. B.

'Lactea' (Marliac 1907) Fragrant variety, opening apricot blush becoming white as the flowers age; green sepal reverses. B.

'Loose' is an American variety reminiscent of the tropicals. The flowers are pure white, stellate and borne 20–25 cm (8–10 in) above water level; they are 12.5–17.5 cm (5–7 in) in diameter and sweetly scented. B.

'Marliacea Albida' (Marliac 1880) Free-flowering, fragrant variety with snow white flowers 10–12.5 cm (4–5 in) across. A.

N. odorata, the fragrant water lily of North America, is the parent of a good many garden hybrids. They are all fragrant, but produce fewer blooms per season than the Marliacs, and should be given a fair amount of room, as, once established, they become very prolific. The type has pure white flowers and pale green foliage. B.

N. odorata 'Gigantea' (*N.o.* 'Maxima'), also known as the 'Southern Odorata'. The pond lily of North America with large white fragrant flowers

10–17.5 cm (4–7 in) across and deep green leaves which are purplish beneath. Needs deep water. A.

'Pygmaea Alba', almost identical with and by some authorities considered merely a form of N. *tetragona*. Small, white flowers which set seeds and plants are easily reproduced from them. C.

'Souvenir de Fridolfing' (Marliac) Large white flowers with golden stamens. A and B.

N. *tetragona* is the baby of the hardy species water lilies. It is widely distributed, being found in various forms in India, Australia, America, China, Siberia and Japan. It was first introduced into Britain as long ago as 1805 and has proved quite hardy where there is 20–22.5 cm (8–9 in) of water covering the crown. The small white flowers are very dainty, about the size of a silver dollar or crown piece, and seed freely. Seed sown in March will produce flowering youngsters the same season. The olive-green foliage is, according to Rein, gathered in the bud stage, pickled with vinegar and eaten by the Japanese. C.

N. *tuberosa* North American species, pure white but rather robust. A better plant is the variety known as 'Richardsonii' (Richardson), pure white, slightly fragrant with green sepals but less free-flowering than 'Gladstoniana'. A.

'Virginalis' (Marliac 1910) is one of the most beautiful with very large, pure white flowers nearly 30 cm (12 in) across, which have shell-like, slightly incurved petals. Very fragrant. B.

PINK AND RED FLOWERS

N. *alba rubra* The rare red form of the European N. *alba*. Blooms pink on opening, deepening to red with age. It was introduced to Britain in 1875 and is responsible for the red in many of Marliac's hybrids. Needs very cold water. A.

'Amabilis' also known as 'Pink Marvel' (Marliac 1921) Stellate flowers of soft salmon pink, deepening to rose with age; golden stamens. A.

'Arc-en-Ciel' (Marliac 1901) Sweetly scented flowers of salmon-white with rose splashed sepals. Foliage green blotched with bronze, white, rose and purple. A and B.

'Arethusa' (Dreer) Cup-shaped blooms of deep red with crimson centre. B.

'Atropurpurea' (Marliac 1901) One of the darkest reds available, large open flowers; young foliage purple passing to green with maturity. B.

'Attraction' (Marliac 1910) has large glowing, garnet-red flowers, 17.5–20 cm (7–8 in) across; mahogany stamens tipped with yellow. Very popular variety. A and B.

'Baroness Orczy' (Marliac 1937) Good shape, rosy-pink flowers. B.

'Bateau' A new variety from Marliac, full double, carmine rose flowers. B.

'Brakleyi Rosea' Splendid deep rose-pink variety, the blooms held just above the water level; flowers fragrant, golden stamens. B.

'Caroliniana' a natural hybrid between N. *odorata* 'Rosea' and N. *tuberosa* from the U.S. Flowers sweetly scented, soft rose-pink with yellow stamens. C.

'Caroliniana Perfecta' (Marliac 1893) has salmon-pink flowers, which are deep rose in 'Caroliniana Rosea'. C.

'Charles de Meurville' (Marliac), a very vigorous variety with wine-red blooms up to 25 cm (10 in) across. A.

'Chateau le Rouge' a superb variety with very large flowers of intense dark red. A.

'Comte de Bouchard' (Lagrange 1904) bears purplish-rose flowers with apricot stamens. The blooms are small, but very free. B.

'Conqueror' (Marliac 1910) A most attractive variety which blooms prolifically. The inside of the sepals is white and contrasts with the petals which are of a brilliant red shade flecked with white. B.

'Darwin' (Marliac 1909) bears variegated flowers of a red shade, heavily striped with white. It is sweetly scented; the foliage is green. B.

'Eburnea' (Marliac) bears white flowers overlaid with green and pink lines; they are well shaped and sweetly scented. The foliage is bright green. B.

'Ellisiana' (Marliac 1896) has small garnet-red flowers with orange-red stamens and green leaves. This variety is inclined to fasciation. B and C.

'Escarboucle' also called 'Aflame' (Marliac 1909) One of the best varieties for large or medium pools. Free-flowering, large, wine-crimson blooms as big as tea plates; yellow-tipped reddish stamens. A and B.

'Esmeralda' (Marliac 1912) bears stellate flowers of a red hue, variegated with white. B.

'Eucharist' (Marliac 1912) carries large open flowers of a soft rose shade, heavily flecked and splashed with white. B.

'Eugenia de Land' gives medium sized, stellate flowers standing several inches above water level; they are of a rich pink shade with golden-yellow stamens. B.

'Fabiola' (Marliac 1913) A meritorious variety with a long flowering season. The blooms are large and open, of a rich pink shade with mahogany stamens. The foliage is green. B.

'Fire Crest' is an American variety with fragrant, deep pink flowers. The petals lie widely open so that the red-tipped stamens stand erect in the centre. This gives them a unique appearance and probably suggests the colloquial name. B.

'Formosa' (Marliac 1909) bears soft rose flowers which pass to a deeper shade with age; rich golden stamens and green foliage. B.

'Froebeli' (Froebel) A first-rate variety for a small pool or tub garden; very free-flowering, easy to grow and of a blood-red shade. C.

'Fulva' (Marliac 1894) A rather weak grower with thin reddish-yellow flowers. C.

'Galatée' (Marliac 1909) has soft rose flowers, flecked and spotted with white. The foliage is green heavily variegated with purple. B.

'Gloriosa' (Marliac 1896) A great favourite both in America and Europe with 15–17.5 cm (6–7 in) flowers of carmine-rose which deepen in colour as the blooms age. Semi-double; will also thrive in light shade. B.

'Goliath' (Marliac 1912) Unusual long-petalled, tulip-shaped flowers of white tinged with pink, also conspicuous white stamens and orange-red petaloids. A.

'Grésille' (Marliac) Large cerise-red flowers with red stamens tipped with gold. B.

'J. C. N. Forestier' (Marliac) bears flowers standing well above water level. On first opening they are of a soft copper-rose shade, with orange-red stamens, but the colour is intensified as the blooms mature. B.

'James Brydon' (Dreer) A very fine American variety bearing cup-shaped flowers of a rich carmine-red. This is one of the finest of the hardy water lilies, well adapted for natural or artificial pools; it will succeed in partially shaded positions. B.

'James Hudson' (Marliac 1912) carries large stellate flowers of a purplish-crimson shade; green foliage. B.

'Labeaugère' (Marliac) has broad rosy crimson petals which are deeper in colour towards the base. Yellow stamens. B.

'Larroque' (Marliac) Large flowers with long, clear rose petals. A.

'Laydekeri' These small-growing hybrid water lilies were all raised by M. Marliac who probably used *N. tetragona* as one of the parents, for, although differing in size and colour, there is a distinct resemblance in the shape of the flowers. Their free-flowering propensities ensure them great popularity; it is not uncommon to find as many as 50 to 60 blooms out at once on a well established plant of 'Laydekeri Purpurata'. As a general rule the foliage is not large and is of a uniform shade of green. C.

'Laydekeri Fulgens' Brilliant crimson-magenta with fiery-red stamens. C.

'Laydekeri Lilacea' Fragrant blossoms of soft rose-lilac which deepen with age to bright carmine. The stamens are yellow. C.

'Laydekeri Purpurata' is the freest flowering form of the group and is in bloom throughout the whole season. It is rosy-crimson, slightly spotted and flecked with white. B and C.

'Laydekeri Rosea' is perhaps the loveliest of all the Laydekeris but unfortunately is almost, if not quite, lost to cultivation. The fragrant deep rose blossoms, of a perfect cup-shape, float flat upon the water and are in character throughout the summer. B and C.

'Leviathan' (Marliac 1910) A strong grower with large fragrant flowers of a soft pink shade and plain-green leaves. A.

'Livingstone' (Marliac 1909) has long petals which bear a certain resemblance to the flowers of a tulip; they are delicately scented, of a bright red shade flecked with white. The stamens are mahogany-red. B.

'Lucida' (Marliac 1894) A strong grower with star-shaped flowers of pale pink which deepen with age to rosy-vermilion, orange stamens; large olive-green leaves marbled bronze-maroon. B.

'Lusitania' (Marliac 1912) is deep rose with brilliant mahogany stamens; the

A well-planted bog garden, the interest sustained by clever placing of hostas and the variegated foliage of *Iris pseudacorus* 'Variegata'.

Eichhornia crassipes, a spectacular floating aquatic which bobs about like a cork and bears spikes of blue hyacinth-like flowers in summer.

young foliage is purple but becomes green when mature. A.

'Marguerite Laplace' (Marliac 1913) A meritorious variety with 15–17.5 cm (6–7 in) saucer-shaped rose flowers which are deeper coloured at the petal extremities. Blooms freely all summer. A and B.

'Marliacea Carnea' also known as 'Morning Glory' (Marliac 1887) Large, 12.5–15 cm (5–6 in), star-shaped, flesh-pink flowers with a rosy tinge at the base of sepals and petals. Reliable and free-flowering. A and B.

'Marliacea Rosea' (Marliac 1887) Sometimes called 'Cornea'. Similar to preceding except for the rich deep rose colour of the blooms, which are also fragrant. An adaptable plant suitable for medium or large pools, but divide every fourth year. A and B.

'Marliacea Rubra Punctata' (Marliac 1889) Smaller flowers than preceding and blooms more globular; deep rosy-carmine. B.

'Marliacea Flammea' (Marliac 1894) has olive-green foliage prettily mottled with chestnut-brown; amaranth flowers are shaded and flecked with white. B.

'Marliacea Ignea' (Marliac 1893) produces flowers 10–12.5 cm (4–5 in) across, of a vivid carmine shade with glaring red anthers. The plant is extremely free, and bears rich bronze leaves which turn with age to dark green mottled with brown blotches. B.

'Maréchal Pétain' (Marliac) A rose-coloured variety of unusual beauty. A.

'Masaniello' (Marliac 1908) Another popular variety; deep rose, sweetly scented flowers, very free in growth and bloom. A and B.

'Maurice Laydeker' (Marliac) bears small red flowers and is an excellent variety for small pools. C.

'Mme de Bonseigneur' (Marliac) Soft rose, striped and streaked with a deeper shade of rose. B.

'Mme Maurice Laydeker' (Marliac) bears globular flowers of a uniform shade of rose-cerise. B.

'Mme Wilfron Gonnêre' (Marliac) bears large, double rose-pink flowers and green foliage. B.

'Mrs Richmond' (Marliac 1910) bears immense, globular, deep pink flowers and green leaves. A robust variety. A and B.

'Mrs C. W. Thomas' (Johnson) is an American hybrid with very fine semi-double shell-pink flowers. The plant is very free, fragrant and easily grown. B.

'Murillo' (Marliac 1910) has star-shaped flowers with pointed petals, floating flat upon the water. These are bright rose, the outer ring of petals being flushed with white. B.

'Neptune' (Marliac 1914) Deep rose-crimson, stellate flowers with rosy stamens. Young foliage purple, changing with age to olive-green. B.

'Newton' (Marliac 1910) has star-shaped, brilliant rosy-vermilion flowers with long orange stamens. The blooms are shapely and tend to stand above the water. B.

'Odalisque' (Marliac 1908) has rhizomatous rootstocks with a profusion of soft pink flowers which deepen with age to rose; orange stamens, flowers standing several inches above the water. B and C.

N. odorata 'Helen Fowler' has blooms that may reach 22.5 cm (9 in) across and are of a deep rose shade; strongly almond scented. B.

N. odorata 'Luciana' (Dreer) Stellate flowers of a rich glowing rose colour. It is sweetly scented with green foliage. B.

N. odorata rosea is the Cape Cod pond water lily. It bears intense rose-pink flowers, which deepen in colour towards the centre, and yellow stamens. The foliage is purplish-green. It is found locally in N. America. Millspough (1893, in 'Pink Water Lilies', *Torrey Botanical Bulletin*) gives the following note concerning this plant: 'On a plat of low bottom land near Buffalo, Putnam County, the plough turns up a large number of small tubers each season that the soil is cultivated. These, planted in tubs, produce, much to the astonishment of the neighbourhood, beautiful deep pink water lilies. How long the bottom has been drained is not known, but the evidence adduced by the fact above stated of the existence of a pond here, certainly over a century ago, is very interesting.' B.

N. odorata 'Turicensis', free-flowering form with soft rose blossoms, sweetly scented. B and C.

N. odorata 'W. B. Shaw' (Dreer) is a very desirable water lily with good-sized, cup-shaped flowers of a delicate pink. The inner zone of the corolla is marked with deeper colouration and affords a delightful contrast to the rest of the petal. B and C.

'Pearl of the Pool' (Slocum 1945) Uniform shade of soft rosy-pink with yellow stamens, good shape, green leaves. B.

'Pink Opal', stellate flowers of coral-pink several inches above water level. They make good cut blooms. B.

'Pink Sensation' (Slocum 1964) A free-flowering, fragrant, rich pink variety with stellate flowers. Inner sepals deep rosy-red. Blooms stay open longer than most hardy lilies. B.

'Princess Elizabeth' (Perry 1935) This pretty hybrid is a seedling of 'Brakleyi Rosea'. It is of a charming peach-blossom hue which deepens in intensity with maturity; the plant is free-flowering and fragrant. B.

N. pygmaea 'Rubra' The blooms and leaves of this variety are a good deal bigger, 6.2 cm ($2\frac{1}{2}$ in), than the rest of the pygmy forms, although the plant does not seem to become larger from one year's end to another. The flowers open rose, the outer petals being white lightly flushed with pink, and eventually change to a rich garnet-red. The foliage is green with a reddish undersurface. C.

'Picciola' (Marliac 1913) Very strong-growing plant with abundant amaranth-crimson flowers often 22.5–25 cm (9–10 in) across. A.

'Rene Gerard' (Marliac 1914) Stellate flowers frequently 22.5 cm (9 in) across of rich rose, flecked and striped with crimson; very free-flowering. B.

'Robinsoniana' (Marliac 1895) Produces fine flowers of unique colouring. They are yellow, heavily overlaid with rose-vermilion: open from nine in the morning until six at night. The foliage is spotted with maroon. B.

'Rose Arey' A very fine form with large stellate flowers in which the petals are slightly incurved. This is of a uniform shade of rich rose-pink, very free, and delightfully fragrant. B.

'Rose Nymphe' (Junge) One of the most beautiful. Large, open flowers, 15–17.5 cm (6–7 in) across, an exquisite shade of deep rose; fragrant and produced in abundance from early spring until late autumn. B.

'Sanguinea' (Marliac 1894) is a brilliant shade of crimson-carmine with orange-red stamens. The leaves are olive-green, beautifully blotched with brown. B.

'Senegal' (Marliac) Large, brilliant red. A and B.

'Somptuosa' (Marliac 1909) Throws globular flowers of a rose-pink shade; it is very fragrant and has orange stamens. B.

'Souvenir de Jules Jacquier' (Marliac 1921) is of vigorous constitution, and bears globular flowers a uniform shade of mauve-pink. B.

'Splendide' (Marliac) Very large red flowers; one of the best in this colour. A and B.

'Suavissima' (Marliac 1899) Fragrant, rosy-pink flowers carried just above the water. C.

N. tuberosa 'Rosea', a vigorous variety with soft pink, fragrant flowers and light green leaves. A.

N. tuberosa 'Rubra' (Sturtevant 1901) Rosy-red flowers, 12.5–17.5 cm (5–7 in) across, with ruby red stamens. Slightly fragrant but a shy bloomer. A.

'Venusta' (Marliac 1910) Open flowers a uniform shade of rich pink. B.

'Vésuve' (Marliac 1906) Fiery amaranth flowers with bright red stamens, blooms large and open, 17.5–20 cm (7–8 in) across. B and C.

'William Doogue' (Dreer 1899) An American variety with large shell-pink flowers which pass to white with age. Free-flowering. A and B.

'William Falconer' (Dreer) American lily with very dark red flowers 15–17.5 cm (6–7 in) across, and yellow stamens. Young foliage red but becoming green with age. A and B.

YELLOW FLOWERS

'Colonel Welch' (Marliac) A shy-flowering but vigorous variety with canary-yellow blooms raised on short stems just above the water. A.

'Marliacea Chromatella', also called 'Golden Cup' (Marliac 1877) Soft canary-yellow flowers of fine rounded shape with bright yellow stamens. One of the best and freest flowering in this shade. Chocolate blotched foliage. B.

N. mexicana (N. flava) is a species from Florida and Mexico which is not quite so hardy as most water lilies. Foliage is green, heavily blotched with purple and with a reddish under-surface; flowers bright yellow standing several inches above water level. Overwinter away from frost. C.

'Moorei' (raised in Adelaide, Australia 1900) Very similar to 'Marliacea

Chromatella' except that the foliage is less heavily blotched. B.

N. odorata 'Sulphurea' (Marliac 1879) Deep sulphur-yellow flowers standing above water level; a hybrid between *N. odorata* and *N. mexicana*. The leaves are blotched with chocolate coloured markings. C.

N. pygmaea 'Helvola' (Marliac 1879) is the prettiest pygmy form and a hybrid between *N. tetragona* and *N. flava*. The tiny, star-shaped flowers 2.5 cm (1 in) across are a delightful soft sulphur shade, produced in abundance throughout the season. The olive-green foliage is prettily marked with brown and maroon blotches. It is a dainty little plant, worthy of cultivation in every water garden. C.

'Sunrise' This American variety is undoubtedly the finest yellow yet introduced—of a glorious sunny shade with golden filaments. The individual blooms are very large and fragrant; the foliage is green with a red under-surface, flecked with brown. B.

FLOWERS WITH CHANGEABLE COLOURS
'Andreana' (Marliac 1895) Compact but free-flowering variety with dark red flecked blooms overlaid with yellow; foliage blotched with red. B.

'Aurora' (Marliac 1895) A remarkable form on account of the varying changes of colour throughout successive stages of growth. Opening yellow, the flowers become orange the next day, finally turning dark red by the third. The plant is free-flowering and has prettily mottled foliage. C.

'Chrysantha' (Marliac 1905) Small flowers of reddish-yellow which change to cinnabar-red with age. Free-flowering but rather insignificant. B and C.

'Comanche' (Marliac 1908) Flowers open rich rose overlaid apricot, passing to deep coppery-red as they mature. This shade in conjunction with the orange stamens affords a distinct colouration feature among hardy water lilies. The young foliage is purple passing to green with age. B.

'Graziella' (Marliac 1904) bears pretty reddish-yellow flowers, which are inclined to become lighter with age; the foliage is heavily variegated with purple. This variety is free-flowering and an excellent form for tub culture. C.

'Iga Erfurt' (Forst 1961) A very pretty pygmy lily with changeable flower colours. These open yellow and deepen to copper-red. Leaves green, mottled chocolate-red. C.

'Indiana' (Marliac 1912) Shows a great deal of variation in the flowers. These open orange-red, gradually darkening with age until the mature flower is brilliant rich copper-red. Foliage heavily spotted and mottled with purple. B and C.

'Lucida' (Marliac 1894) Flowers of a rosy-vermilion with a darker centre. The plant is free in growth and flower, and has purple variegated foliage. B and C.

'Paul Hariot' (Marliac 1905) On opening, the flower is a delicate apricot-yellow; the next day it is orange-pink and this deepens almost to red on the ensuing days. The foliage is green, attractively spotted with maroon; the plant is of small habit but very free-flowering. B.

'Phoebus' (Marliac 1909) Flowers inclined to be small, yellow with red suffusion, passing to coppery-red; fiery orange stamens, leaves green heavily mottled chocolate brown. B.

'Sioux' (Marliac 1908) is another variety which changes colour. Opening soft yellow suffused with red, it develops to an attractive shade of reddish-copper. B.

'Solfatare' (Marliac 1906) bears stellate flowers of a yellow tint flushed with rose; the foliage is heavily mottled with maroon. B.

Tropical species
(All day-blooming unless otherwise stated)

N. ampla, white with stellate flowers to 12.5 cm (5 in) across standing well out of the water, from tropical and sub-tropical America. Very floriferous and frequently planted in display pools in tropical countries.

N. caerulea, the blue lotus of the Nile. Widespread through Northern and Central Africa with pale blue flowers on long stems. These have black spots on the sepals and are fragrant. Leaves green and wavy edged.

N. capensis, Cape blue water lily. Flowers sky-blue with paler centres, 15–20 cm (6–8 in) across; var. zanzibariensis has larger blooms up to 30 cm (12 in) of a deeper blue. There are also cultivars with pale blue 'Azurea' or pink 'Rosea' flowers.

N. colorata, an African species with small but broad petalled purplish petals.

N. flavivirens, frog water lily. Mexican species, very vigorous, stellate white flowers 15–20 cm (6–8 in) across, golden stamens and green sepals; sweet smelling.

N. gigantea. Magnificent Australian species with very large 30 cm (12 in) powder-blue flowers filled with masses of incurved, golden stamens; green foliage which is purplish beneath. There is also a white form.

N. heudelotii from central Africa bears small bluish-white flowers about 5 cm (2 in) across. Has been used as a pollen parent for cultivars by George Pring but is rarely grown for its own sake.

N. lotus, the white lotus of the Nile, with broad petalled flowers 12.5–25 cm (5–10 in) across, opening in the evening. Var. dentata (N. dentata of some authors) has narrower petals, and undersides of leaves are densely hairy.

N. micrantha, a viviparous species with small bluish-white flowers clear of the water. Often the juvenile and parent plants bloom together while still attached. Shallow water is essential.

N. rubra A night-flowering species from India with 30–45 cm (12–18 in) reddish-brown leaves and bright red flowers with cinnabar stamens.

N. stellata, the blue lotus of India, and very like the African N. caerulea except that the leaves have pinkish-purple undersides.

Tropical water lily cultivars
(*Day blooming*)
'African Gold' (Pring 1941) Rich deep yellow, small leaves.

'Afterglow' (Randig) An unusual bicolour with orange, yellow and pink flowers, golden centred; green leaves.

'American Beauty' (Pring 1941) Flowers fuchsia red with lemon centres, 15–25 cm (6–10 in) across; large, wavy-edged green leaves.

'August Koch' (Koch) A viviparous variety useful for the indoor pool owing to its continuous bloom throughout summer and winter. The flowers, of a pleasing shade of blue, are frequently 17.5–20 cm (7–8 in) in diameter and make good cut blooms.

'Aviator Pring' (Pring) A magnificent deep yellow, flowers up to 30 cm (12 in) across on long stout stems. Probably the best in this shade.

'Bagdad' (Pring 1941) Short-stemmed, flat flowers of wistaria blue with yellow stamens, leaves blotched with chocolate brown, viviparous.

'Blue Beauty' (University of Pennsylvania) Often called N. *pennsylvania* but of hybrid origin. Deep blue flowers 25–30 cm (10–12 in) across, golden stamens tipped with violet.

'Bob Trickett' (Pring 1948) Flowers cup-shaped, rich blue with blue-tipped yellow stamens; 25–35 cm (10–14 in) across.

'Céleste' (Pring 1941) Rich violet with clear golden stamens and purple-striped buds. Occasionally viviparous.

'Daisy' (Pring 1934) Flowers white, large, saucer-shaped, golden centre; leaves mottled with brown. Viviparous.

'Director George T. Moore' (Pring 1941) Deep rich purple with golden centres to flowers; leaves flecked with purple. Free flowering and prodigal of tubers.

'Edward C. Eliot' (Pring 1923) Pale pink flowers with yellow stamens tipped with pink; frequently 20–25 cm (8–10 in) in diameter.

'General Pershing' (Pring 1917) Large flowers of warm pink; yellow stamens lightly tipped with rose; flowers fragrant, remaining open, and borne 30 cm (12 in) above water.

'Henry Shaw' (Pring 1917) Open, saucer-shaped flowers of light campanula-blue, and green foliage. One of the finest of the day-bloomers.

'Isabelle Pring' (Pring 1941) Full petalled white, fragrant, with light green buds, very large green leaves; viviparous.

'Judge Hitchcock' (Pring 1941) Cup-shaped, violet flowers with blue-tipped, golden stamens; small mottled leaves, purplish beneath.

'Midnight' (Pring 1941) Small but numerous flowers, deep purple with very small golden centres.

'Mrs Edwards Whitaker' (Pring 1917) Pale lavender flowers over 30 cm (12 in) across, the bright yellow stamens forming a pleasant contrast.

'Mrs Woodrow Wilson' (Pring 1917) A viviparous variety with lavender-blue flowers of large size and firm texture; the foliage is green.

'Mrs George H. Pring' (Pring 1922) Pure white flowers up to 32.5 cm (13 in) across with yellow stamens; fragrant and plentiful.

'Mrs Martin E. Randig' (Randig) Very large, rich cobalt blue flowers; viviparous.

'Panama Pacific' (Pring) A widely planted viviparous variety. The deep blue flowers develop reddish-purple shades with maturity, producing a mottled effect.

'Persian Lilac' (Pring 1934) Lilac-pink flowers of moderate size; golden stamens tipped pink; smallish leaves with red undersides.

'Pink Platter' (Pring 1934) Large, flat flowers of rosy pink with pink-tipped, golden stamens; viviparous.

'Rio Rita' (Pring 1934) A brilliant pink, almost red variety with wide open, moderate-sized flowers which have pink-tipped, golden stamens; leaves small, red beneath, lightly speckled with reddish brown above. Occasionally viviparous.

'St Louis' (Pring 1932) Very large, light yellow flowers with deeper coloured stamens; blooms star-shaped. This was the first good yellow.

'Shell Pink' (Pring 1941) Clear pink flowers with green buds and chocolate-blotched leaves.

'Stella Gurney' (Gurney) Large, stellate, light pink flowers.

'Sunbeam' (Pring 1941) Viviparous variety with large, deep yellow flowers and purple-striped buds.

'Talisman' (Pring 1941) Large, star-shaped, soft yellow flowers flushed with bright pink; small leaves, reddish beneath.

'Wild Rose' (Pring 1941) A viviparous plant with solid, large petalled bright pink flowers which have pink-tipped stamens.

'William Stone' (Tricker) Large, violet-blue flowers, shaded amaranth.

Night-blooming cultivars
(*None of these is viviparous*)
'B. C. Berry' (Pring 1922) Large, 20–22.5 cm (8–9 in), shallow flowers, amaranth purple with brighter petal bases; leaves indented at margins.

'Emily Grant Hutchings' (Pring 1922) Very large flowers of pinkish-red, cup-shaped.

'Frank Trelease' (Pring 1922) Popular on account of its deep colour. Huge, deep crimson flowers, 20–25 cm (8–10 in) across, with deep reddish-brown stamens; shy flowering.

'H. C. Haarstick' (Pring 1922) Copper-coloured leaves with indented margins and fragrant, deep rose-pink flowers held well above the water, 25–30 cm (10–12 in) across.

'James Gurney' (Gurney 1948) Fragrant, deep rose flowers, 25–30 cm (10–12 in) across, which deepen in colour with age. Leaves very large with fluted margins.

'Mrs George C. Hitchcock' (Pring 1926) Large rose-pink flowers with orange stamens.

'Missouri' (Pring 1930) Huge, up to 35 cm (14 in) blooms, pure white with many broad petals; very free, of strong constitution with large, mottled leaves which are indented on the margins.

'O'Marana' (Bisset) Glowing red, 25–30 cm (10–12 in) flowers, which have a faint white line running down the centre of each petal.

6

Other deep-water ornamentals

Although water lilies are undoubtedly the most important aquatics which grow in deep water there are several others commonly planted as ornamentals in tropical and sub-tropical countries. Where frosts occur however these must be kept all the time under glass or treated as annuals to be discarded after flowering, or else lifted and brought inside for the winter.

Included among them are nelumbos and the giant victorias. Nuphars however will tolerate very cold conditions, many being native to northern Europe and North America.

Victorias

Victorias were first found in Bolivia by the botanist Haenke in 1801. Ten years later Aimé Bonpland came across others near the town of Corrientes in Argentina; and then in 1936 Sir Robert Schomburgk found plants growing in the river Berbice in British Guiana (now Guyana) and sent seeds and dried specimens to Kew Gardens in England. There then arose great rivalry and competition among the botanic gardens and private establishments of Europe, all of whom wanted to be the first to flower this so called mystery plant. There were many abortive attempts until in 1849, after several failures, Joseph Paxton, gardener to the Duke of Devonshire, obtained flowers in a specially built glasshouse at Chatsworth House in Derbyshire. The botanist John Lindley then visited Chatsworth and drew up a descriptive account of the plant, which he named *Victoria regia* in honour of Queen Victoria. This name has now been changed to *Victoria amazonica*. Another species *V. cruziana* from Paraguay is similar but somewhat hardier.

The victoria is known locally in South America by various native names such as Yrupe, Morinqua, Dachocho, Irupe and Murura. Yrupe, literally translated, means 'water platter'—surely an excellent title for the huge leaves, up to 2 m (6 ft) in diameter, lie flat on the water with their edges upturned to a height of 5–20 cm (2–8 in). Although thin, they are strengthened by a framework of

45

veins which makes them capable of sustaining weights of up to 65 kg (143 lb). This is probably the reason why so many illustrations portray a child—frequently in Victorian dress—standing or sitting on one of the leaves. The flowers are nocturnal, 30–40 cm (12–14 in) in diameter; white on first opening but changing to pink and then purplish-red on successive evenings. They have a sweet pineapple-like fragrance, and all parts of the plant—flowers, stems and leaves—are armed with sharp spines.

Although victorias are perennial they are invariably treated as annuals when cultivated. In Europe they are rarely grown except in botanic gardens, but in parts of the United States as well as Central and South America they provide striking features in ornamental lakes and pools. The same mixture of heavy loam and fertilizer required by hardy and tropical water lilies is suitable for victorias; approximately 0.30 m^3 (a cubic foot) of the mixture being necessary for each plant and a growing area at least 6 m (20 ft) in diameter.

The dark brown, pea-sized seeds germinate best when two to three years old. These are sown in early spring in shallow pots of equal parts sand and loam, then covered with about twice their depth of this mixture, before being submerged under 7.5 cm (3 in) of water and kept in a temperature of 27°C (80°F) to germinate. They are then gradually potted on in richer soil (containing a larger proportion of loam) until they are ready to go outside in mid-summer. By that time the leaves will be about 30 cm (1 ft) in diameter. After the first frost remove any seed pods—using gloves since these are as prickly as cacti—and keep them in a warm greenhouse until the seeds separate from the husks. This usually takes about six weeks. They should then be stored in boxes of moist sand, in a temperature of 15°C (60°F) until the following spring.

Euryales

Until victorias were discovered, *Euryale ferox*, the gorgon plant, was thought to be the largest aquatic plant in existence. It is native to S.E. Asia and China, where it has been cultivated for centuries as a food plant, and has flat leaves, 1.2–1.5 m (4–5 ft) across, which do not turn up at the edges, and small, 5 cm (2 in) violet-blue flowers. In Japan the young stems and roots are esteemed as a vegetable and the farinaceous seeds eaten when baked or dried to make a starchy flour. The plant is hardy in southern Europe and northern Africa, also in parts of the United States such as Kansas and Florida, where it often resows itself annually.

Nelumbos

Nelumbos are native to both the old world and the new. *N. nucifera* from the Orient is the famous sacred lotus of the Hindus; Buddha is supposed to have been born in the heart of this lotus. It could also be the sacred lotus of the Nile,

thought by scholars to have been introduced into Egypt from India about
525 BC at the time of the Persian invasion. Herodotus called this plant the rose
lily and described its seed pods as being 'in form very like a wasps' nest, in which
there are many berries fit to be eaten'. Lotus seeds are still eaten when dried,
salted or candied, but in ancient times they were also ground into flour and made
into loaves with milk or water. This habit, and the mode of sowing, which
consisted of wrapping the seeds in balls of clay and throwing them into water,
may be the origin of the text 'Cast thy bread upon the waters, for thou shalt find
it after many days'.

Lotus rhizomes are eaten as a vegetable in the far East and also candied as a
sweetmeat. The stamens are used to flavour tea in Indo-China, and the leaves
boiled as a vegetable. Nelumbos are commonly portrayed on porcelain, glass
and murals in the East; poems are written about the plant, and the Victorian
Order of the Star of India is comprised of a lotus flower, the rose of England,
and two crossed palm branches.

Unfortunately, this historic plant is not hardy in Britain and northern
Europe, although plants may be grown outdoors in the south of Europe—there
is a big collection at Pallanza in Italy—also in warmer parts of the United States.
It is a difficult plant to establish but may be grown in a tub or large container,
taken inside in late autumn before frost damages the crown. Keep the soil moist
but not wet in winter in a temperature around 4°C (39°F). Good rich soil, as
prescribed for water lilies, is essential, with a 5–7.5 cm (2–3 in) layer of well
decayed cow manure over the base of the container. Place the banana-shaped
rhizome horizontally in the soil with the growing point exposed and weigh
the tuber down (without touching the growing point) under a piece of rock.
Cover the soil with a layer of sand (except for the growing tip), then add
5–7.5 cm (2–3 in) of water and set the tub in a warm, sunny situation. Damage
to the growing tip is nearly always fatal so great care must be taken.

Nelumbo nucifera (*Nelumbium speciosum*) has large, round, 30–90 cm
(1–3 ft), glaucous green, water-repellent leaves poised like parasols on stout
stalks above the water, and large, fragrant, poppy-shaped flowers up to 30 cm
(12 in) across. These are pink or rose or occasionally white, with plenty of
golden stamens surrounding an ovary shaped like the rose of a watering can.
Cultivars include: 'Mrs Perry Slocum', which opens deep pink, becomes pink
and yellow the next day, and creamy-yellow with a pink edging the third;
'Pekinensis Rubra', rosy-carmine; 'Rosea Plena', double rose pink; and 'Alba
Striata', white edged with carmine.

N. lutea is the North American water chinquapin, a hardier but less attractive
species with pale yellow flowers up to 25 cm (10 in) in diameter and 30–60 cm
(1–2 ft) circular leaves.

Propagation of nelumbos is normally effected by division of the rhizomes, or
by rolling the seeds (after scarifying the hard outer coats to facilitate germina-
tion) in balls of clay, and dropping them into pans of soil covered with water.

Nuphars

Nuphars are hardy, robust plants akin but inferior to hardy water lilies. They have strong creeping rootstocks, up to 2 m (6 ft) long and 10 cm (4 in) thick, with prominent scars from old leaf stalks, scattered roots, and both submerged and floating leaves. The former develop only in deep water, although they are present for a time on seedling plants, their thin, filmy, wavy-edged blades looking like underwater ferns. At this stage they are popular for cold water aquaria. The floating foliage is tough and leathery, usually oval to lanceolate with heart-shaped bases. Under crowded conditions these thrust their way upwards and become emerged. The small yellow flowers which are about 5 cm (2 in) in diameter, have five sepals and numerous stamen-like petals surrounding a bottle-shaped fruit which has a vinous odour. This probably accounts for one of its popular names—brandy bottle; others are spatterdock, water collard, cow lily and yellow water lily.

Apart from their use in aquaria, nuphars will grow in positions where nymphaeas normally fail, for example in deep water 1–2 m (3–6 ft) or more, in shade, or in sluggish streams.

Nuphar advena from the eastern states of the U.S.A. is one of the best, with globular, 5 cm (2 in) flowers of rich yellow tinged with green and purple, and oblong oval leaves. A cream and green variegated form is showier. N. *japonica* has large, crisped, submerged leaves and long arrow-shaped floating leaves. The yellow flowers are 5–7.5 cm (2–3 in) across. This Japanese species has a form var. *rubrotinctum* with orange-red flowers. Other yellow-flowered species are N. *subintegerrimum* and N. *oguraense*, both Japanese; N. *pumila* and N. *sagittifolium*, the former rather small with leaves only 12.5 cm (5 in) across, which is widespread in Europe and Asia, the latter from North America; and N. *lutea*, the common yellow lily of Europe, which has leaves up to 40 cm (16 in) long and 30 cm (12 in) across, and bright yellow flowers. All these plants are hardy to frost and grow well in most soils including sandy, loamy or even peaty types.

One other plant, *Aponogeton distachyus*, the water hawthorn (described on p. 52), has floating leaves and flowers. This is hardy outdoors in southern Britain, southern Europe, and Zones 8–10 in North America.

7

Marginal aquatics

Marginal aquatics are plants which grow with their roots submerged in water but have emergent leaves and flowers. Some are extremely ornamental so are usually planted to beautify streamside and pond edges. Others afford shelter for insects and various small creatures which in turn provide food for fishes, and a few are so adaptable that they grow equally well in wet mud or shallow water, a useful habit when you want to mask the artificiality of a man-made pool.

In general deep water is not desirable as this restricts flowering; a depth of 5–10 cm (2–4 in) is suitable for most. Marginal aquatics can be planted in various ways: directly into soil at the base of natural ponds or streams; in pockets or troughs built into the sides of concrete pools; in aquatic baskets with open-work sides; or in pans or large flowerpots which can be stood in the water. The soil need not be rich or it will stimulate too much lush growth. Good heavy loam makes the best planting medium with perhaps a little dried blood or bonemeal added if the loam is poor or stony. As with water lilies, always topdress containers with 1–2 cm ($\frac{1}{2}$–1 in) of washed sand or shingle to prevent fish from disturbing the mud.

Periodic division is necessary with some marginal aquatics, especially those with stoloniferous rootstocks, like typhas, which spread so rapidly that they can become a nuisance, particularly in small pools. Either lift and split these or cut out chunks in early spring. Rampant growers can also be kept in bounds by pushing sheets of slate or tiles vertically downwards into the soil around their roots. All the following are perennial unless otherwise stated.

ACORUS *(Araceae)* sweet flag
A. calamus Eastern Asia; naturalized in Europe, including Britain, and in North America. Height 60–75 cm (2–2$\frac{1}{2}$ ft). A plant often mistaken at first sight for an iris, the leaves and rhizomes being somewhat similar. The flowers, however, reveal its arum nature, being densely packed in short 5–7.5 cm (2–3 in) spikes near the tops of the stems. They are brownish in colour and look rather like small cow's horns, being most plentiful on plants growing in shallow water.

49

The species reached western European gardens in 1574 and Gerard had it in his garden in London by 1596. According to Trimen (1817), not until 1660 was acorus reported as growing wild in Norfolk. There is no doubt that in some localities it was deliberately planted and probably from these has spread to others. The acorus found in Europe does not fruit, which may be because it has all derived from the same clone, nor does it in the older settled parts of North America, to which it was probably introduced from Europe. However, in the northern interior of America, to the east of the Rockies, for example in Minnesota, where it has the appearance of being native, it apparently fruits freely.

In Asia the plant has long been deliberately cultivated for its rootstock and bruised leaves which are very aromatic and have been used for medicinal and toilet purposes; also for flavouring liquids and making into a candied sweet-meat. The powdered root is used for scenting hair pomades, as an ingredient of tooth powders and for cough medicines.

A variety called 'Variegatus' with yellow striped leaves is slower growing and more compact. Height 60–75 cm (2–2½ ft).

A. gramineus, China, Japan. A slender-leaved, almost grassy species without a distinct midrib and of tufted habit. There is a white-striped form called 'Variegatus' 30 cm (12 in) high, and a dwarf oriental variety 'Pusillus' of 7.5–10 cm (3–4 in). These rarely flower in cultivation but are easily reproduced by division in spring.

ALISMA *(Alismataceae)* water plantain

A small group of widely distributed, shallow water aquatics with basal, plantain-like leaves with broad cordate bases and whorled panicles of small, three-petalled rosy-lilac flowers throughout early and late summer. Ribbon-shaped submerged leaves occur before the emergent. Since the plants are apt to spread rapidly from indiscriminate seeding the old flower heads should be regularly removed. Propagate by spring sown seed or division.

A. gramineum, from N. America, N. Europe, Asia and N. Africa, has lanceolate or narrowly oblong leaves up to 50 cm (20 in) long and 30 cm (12 in) panicles of pinkish-white flowers.

A. lanceolatum, Europe including Britain, Asia, has narrower leaves which taper into a stalk and pinker flowers.

A. plantago-aquatica (great water plantain, mad dog weed). North temperate regions. The most robust species with broad, lanceolate, long-stemmed leaves up to 15 cm (6 in) across and 7.5 cm (3 in) wide; flowers pale lilac or whitish on whorls up to 60 cm (2 ft) high. It will only flower well in shallow water.

ANEMOPSIS *(Saururaceae)* yerba mansa, apache beads

A. californica N. America from California and Nevada to Texas. A handsome plant native to wet alkaline soil with long-stalked, basal, oblong-elliptic leaves

Top: *Butomus umbellatus* (p. 55), bottom left: *Calla palustris* (p. 56), right: *Aponogeton distachyus* (p. 52).

to 17.5 cm (7 in) with 3.5 cm (1½ in) conical spikes of white flowers in early summer, each of which is subtended by a white bract. General height 45–60 cm (1½–2 ft). The pungent aromatic rootstocks have medicinal properties and are regularly sold in Mexican markets for the relief of colds. They are also made into beads and strung into necklaces as a specific against malaria. Propagate by division in spring.

APONOGETON (Aponogetonaceae)

A. distachyus (*A. distachyos*, *A. distachyon*) (cape pondweed, water hawthorn). The water hawthorn owes its name to the rich vanilla scent emitted by the flowers. This is particularly marked on still evenings and although most of the blooms appear in summer it is not unusual to find stray flowers in early winter. The plant is South African, with a chestnut-sized tuber from which rise strap-shaped floating leaves up to 25 cm (10 in) long and 5 cm (2 in) wide and forked white flowers with black stamens. These also float on the surface so that the plant requires similar planting conditions to water lilies, although shallow water 15–22 cm (6–9 in) produces stronger plants and more flowers. There are several forms in cultivation, e.g. one with larger flowers 'Giganteus' and another with violet undersides to the leaves and violet-tinged flowers called 'Lagrangei'.

The tubers should be planted in heavy loam in pots or boxes and lowered into the pool. In a good summer, water hawthorns set seed freely and if this is collected and sown in shallow pans of soil covered with 1.2 cm (½ in) of water it presents the most convenient method of propagation. The species is hardy in southern Europe, south England, and also in Zone 9 in the U.S.A. In South Africa the flowers and flower stems are eaten, either alone as a vegetable or mixed in stews or 'bredees'. The tubers are also edible and contain starch.

Others may be planted in shallow water in frost free pools outdoors or in tanks in greenhouses. They include the following:

A. desertorum (*A. kraussianus*) from S. Africa, a handsome plant with submerged juvenile leaves, floating, oblong-lanceolate adult leaves to 25 cm (10 in) long on 30 cm (12 in) stems, and forked spikes of creamy-sulphur flowers held well above the water. These are sweetly scented. For many years my father-in-law, Amos Perry, grew a small plant with 1.8 cm (¾ in) twin spikes of lilac-mauve flowers and floating, oblong leaves 2.5–5 cm (1–2 in) long. This was an annual which flowered readily in small pans in a greenhouse when covered with 2.5–5 cm (1–2 in) of water, and reproduced itself each year from seed. This we knew as *A. leptostachyus* var *abyssinicus*, but since *A. leptostachyus* is now considered by Zander and *Hortus Third* to be synonymous with *A. desertorum* it presumably is a form of this species. However, other botanists give it specific rank as *A. abyssinicus*.

There are also a number of aponogetons with mostly submerged leaf blades, although the blooms come above the surface in order to be pollinated. These are useful for tropical aquaria (see pp. 78–79).

Nymphaea 'Panama Pacific'. A day-blooming tropical water lily which produces baby plants on its leaves. The deep blue flowers become reddish-purple with age.

Nymphaea 'Sunrise'. This water lily has large fragrant, and many petalled flowers of sunshine yellow and brown flecked leaves.

BACOPA *(Scrophulariaceae)*

A genus of small plants from warm and tropical parts of the world, many of them weedy but a few worth cultivating as ground-cover over wet soil between taller plants in indoor pools. They are also used as short term submerged plants for tropical aquaria, or, grouped in pans of soil and kept very damp, for home decoration. They like a rich loamy compost and are propagated from cuttings rooted in a temperature of 18–21°C (65–70°F), or by division.

B. amplexicaulis (B. caroliniana, Herpestis amplexicaulis). Tropical and sub-tropical N. America. A handsome, fleshy plant growing 15–45 cm (6–18 in) high, with downy, oval, stemless, 2.5 cm (1 in) leaves tightly clasping the stems, which are lemon scented when bruised, and rich blue, tubular flowers.

B. monnieri (Herpestis monnieri) (water hyssop). Old world tropics. A mat-forming perennial with succulent stems, white to pale blue, axillary flowers and spoon-shaped entire leaves.

BALDELLIA *(Alismataceae)*

B. ranunculoides (Echinodorus ranunculoides) (lesser water plantain). A plant with similar growth habit to alisma and native to western Europe (including Britain), N. Africa, Canaries. Foliage narrow, lance-shaped on long stems; flowers pale purplish borne on lax umbels. Grows 5–20 cm (2–8 in), largely above the water. Propagate by division; the stems frequently root at the nodes.

BRASENIA *(Nymphaeaceae)* water shield or target

B. schreberi (B. peltata), tropical Asia, Africa, Australia, N. America, Cuba. A monotypic genus, the species having small, oval, entire, long-stalked floating leaves, 3–8 cm (1–3 in) long, the undersides of which are reddish and covered with a thick gelatinous matter. In midsummer, the purplish, three-petalled flowers are about 1.2 cm ($\frac{1}{2}$ in) across. In their native haunts the plants, with articulated trailing stems, survive in 1.2–1.8 m (4–6 ft) of water or in slow streams, but in frost-prone countries they are more suitable for indoor pools or cold water aquaria. They need rather acid conditions. Propagated from seed.

BUTOMUS *(Butomaceae)* flowering rush

B. umbellatus, Europe including Britain, Asia. A native of shallow to deep water along wet marshland or streams. The narrow, smooth, rush-like leaves are sheathed at their bases and triangular, all basal and 60–90 cm (2–3 ft) long, up to 1 cm ($\frac{1}{2}$ in) broad. These are bronze-purple when young, becoming rich green. The pink, long petioled, three-petalled flowers come in midsummer, borne in umbels on 90–120 cm (3–4 ft) stems. The baked roots are eaten as food by some Russian races. Propagate by division.

CALDESIA *(Alismataceae)*

C. reniformis (C. parnassifolia var. 'Major'), a smooth annual found in

Australia, China and Japan, in wet ground or shallow fresh water. It has radical, long-stalked, ovate to rounded leaves with 13 parallel nerves, and in late summer shows panicles of white three-petalled flowers on 30–120 cm (1–4 ft) stems. It is doubtfully hardy in cold climates but survives in southern Europe and Zone 9 in the U.S.A. Propagated from seed.

CALLA (Araceae)

C. palustris (bog arum). This is the sole member of a genus belonging to the large family of aroids and native to north temperate and sub-arctic America and northern Asia, although large colonies have also naturalized themselves in Holland, southern Sweden and other parts of northern Europe. The plant grows about 22.5 cm (9 in) high and has a long creeping rhizome bearing smooth, shiny, heart-shaped, dark green, pointed leaves on 5 cm (2 in) long stems and small white arum flowers about late summer. These are reminiscent of the large 'calla' lilies used at Easter for church decoration. If pollinated—which is carried out by water snails, probably attracted by the strong scent of the flowers—the plants go on to produce clusters of small scarlet berries.

The bog arum, being a scrambler, is ideal for masking pond edges, since it wanders with impunity between wet mud and shallow water. It is propagated by cutting the rootstock up into pieces with shoots and roots in early spring. The fresh rhizomes are poisonous but when boiled and ground into flour are used as food by Lapps.

CALTHA (Ranunculaceae) marsh marigold, kingcup, water cowslip, water-blob, meadow rout, water dragon.

C. palustris, a common plant of Arctic and north temperate zones. In Britain it is occasionally found wild in waterlogged meadows where it grows about 30 cm (12 in) tall. It is adaptable, thriving equally well in wet mud or 5 cm (2 in) of water. The smooth, kidney-shaped 5–7.5 cm (2–3 in) leaves and rich golden, 2.5 cm (1 in) buttercup-like flowers are real harbingers of spring for they are the earliest aquatics to bloom in the water garden, being at their best between early spring and summer. The double form 'Flore Pleno' (or 'Monstrosa' in the U.S.A.) is the most decorative, producing such an abundance of bloom as to completely hide the foliage. There is also a white form 'Alba'. The marsh marigold is poisonous to livestock yet in the 19th century country folk in Britain ate the young leaves as a spring salad, also pickled the seeds as a substitute for capers, and dyed their yarn yellow with juice derived from the petals. The plants grow 22.5–30 cm (9–12 in) high and are propagated by division of the roots (for the varieties especially) or from seed sown immediately after harvesting.

Always grow marsh marigolds in clumps for maximum effect and in a position where they can be seen at a distance where, as Tennyson wrote, 'they may shine like fire in swamps and hollows grey'. A good companion for kingcups are water forget-me-nots, Myosotis palustris, their flower colours blending well.

Other calthas sometimes available from nurseries include the following:

C. asarifolia, a N. American (including Alaskan) species with bright yellow flowers.

C. chelidŏnii, a dwarf, 5–10 cm (2–4 in) species from the Canadian Rockies with glossy leaves about 3.5 cm (1½ in) across, forming a rosette and snow-white, golden stamen-filled flowers. This plant needs cool to cold conditions.

C. leptosepala, another white-flowered species from N. America, has narrower petal segments than the preceding species.

C. polypetala, from Bulgaria, is a much larger plant, up to 90 cm (3 ft), of branching habit with many golden flowers which appear several weeks later than *C. palustris*. It spreads by means of stolons so may need restricting in small pools.

COLOCASIA *(Araceae)* taro, coco root, elephant ear

These large-leaved plants from tropical Asia are widely grown in Hawaii and other Pacific islands for food as well as garden decoration, the tubers being more nutritious than potatoes. But they also make attractive ornamentals in warm water pools—either in glasshouses or outdoors in the tropics and sub-tropics. They should be grown in pots of rich soil stood in a few inches of water. The species most favoured for this purpose are *C. antiquorum*, which has stout stems about 100 cm (3½ ft) long and ovate to cordate leaves 50 cm (20 in) long with broadly triangular bases, and *C. esculenta*. Under really warm conditions these produce ill-smelling, mostly yellow, 15–35 cm (6–14 in) arum-like flowers. Varieties of *C. esculenta* have variously marked and coloured leaves. Propagation by division of the tubers or by seed.

COTULA *(Compositae)*

C. coronopifolia (brass buttons). A pretty little plant widely distributed over the southern hemisphere but also naturalized in various warmer parts of the northern hemisphere.

Its smooth, creeping stems, 15–30 cm (6–12 in) high, bear alternate, narrowly lanceolate, smooth, entire or toothed leaves 1.2 cm (½ in) long, which are pleasantly aromatic when crushed, and masses of round, 1.2 cm (½ in) golden flowers like buttons. Damp soil or very shallow water is essential. Propagated from seed.

CYPERUS *(Cyperaceae)*

A large genus, mostly tropical and generally native of wet areas, and occasionally serious weeds of irrigated land. The few ornamentals grown for water gardens are propagated by division or seed or, in the case of *C. papyrus*, by pegging down the old flower heads. In southern Europe *C. esculentus* is cultivated for its edible tubers, which are reputed to taste like potatoes. They are also said to form a passable substitute for coffee and are used in Spain for flavouring ices and

Cyperus papyrus

making a popular beverage known as *chufa*. The dried tuberous roots of others, like *C. rotundus*, the nut grass, are edible, also aromatic and used in perfumery and were once also used by the Scythians for embalming. The roots of *C. longus* have an odour of violets, so used in perfumery and added to lavender water, while ash from *C. haspan* yields salt for some E. African tribes.

Perhaps the most striking species is *C. papyrus*, the plant which furnished the first writing paper of the ancient Egyptians. It is the main constituent of the Sudd on the Nile, and has been plaited into mats and sails, and made into sandals and small boats. For a long time it was thought to be abhorrent to crocodiles, a circumstance—together with its one time abundance in the upper reaches of the Nile—subscribing to the belief that Moses' cradle was fashioned from *C. papyrus*.

C. alternifolius, from Madagascar, is commonly called umbrella grass because of the shape of its umbels of grassy spikelets. It grows 30–75 cm ($1-2\frac{1}{2}$ ft) high and has several forms and subspecies, like *flabelliformis*, with tall to 1.2 m (4 ft), dark green, palm-like umbels of leaves and spikelets. These are utilized by African natives for wickerwork; 'Variegatus' with cream-striped foliage is a popular house plant; and 'Gracilis' is a small, slender form under 45 cm (18 in) in height. None of these is frost hardy.

C. esculentus, from Mediterranean Europe, has round, underground tubers and umbels of straw-coloured spikelets.

C. haspan, S. African, resembles a miniature *C. papyrus*, growing 30–45 cm ($1-1\frac{1}{2}$ ft) tall with a few reddish-brown spikelets on stiff mop-like heads. It makes a pretty pot plant.

C. longus (sweet or English galingale), Europe. Hardy to light frosts this splendid perennial grows 90–120 cm (3–4 ft) tall, with smooth, three-sided leafy stems and arching leafy umbels of reddish-brown spikelets.

C. papyrus (Egyptian paper plant), tropical Africa. A beautiful and graceful species for indoor pools or outdoors in frost free climates. The heavy mop-like heads of spikelets top 4–5 m (12–16 ft) triangular stems. In Uganda natives use the stems to make rafts, binding these tightly together in bundles. It is also used for thatching.

DAMASONIUM *(Alismataceae)*

D. alisma (*D. stellatum*) (thrumwort, starfruit). A west and southern European (including British), low-growing native of still waters, with basal, long-stalked, oval leaves which usually float but are occasionally submerged, and one to three whorls of white, 6 mm ($\frac{1}{4}$ in) flowers with a yellow spot at the base of each petal. These are carried well above the water and develop into six or more pointed fruits arranged in the form of a star.

D. minus, an Australian endemic, is finer with six to ten carpels forming the fruit, white or pale pink flowers, and lanceolate to ovate leaves. Propagated by seed.

DECODON *(Lythraceae)*
D. verticillatus (Nesaea verticillata) (water willow, swamp loosestrife). Purely N. American although fossil remains have been found in Asia and Europe. This short-lived shrub spreads by means of arching branches which root at their tips. It has whorls of narrow, willow-like leaves in the axils of which occur small, tubular, pink flowers in summer. The foliage is green all summer but before falling turns bright crimson. The lower parts of the stems are spongy. Height 1–2.4 m (3–8 ft), propagated by division.

ECHINODORUS (*see* BALDELLIA)

ERIOPHORUM *(Cyperaceae)* cotton grass
Widespread and easily recognized bog plants with very narrow, sedge-like leaves and fluffy heads of silky cotton inflorescence in late summer. At one time this was collected for stuffing pillows and mattresses. All the species mentioned are native to north temperate regions. Propagated by seed or division.

   E. angustifolium (common cotton grass). A perennial 15–45 cm (6–18 in) high with round and grooved, grass-like leaves narrowed to a three-angled point and two to seven nodding spikelets of grassy inflorescence; white with brown bracts.

Eriophorum angustifolium

E. latifolium of tufted habit with broader, flat leaves and 5–12 silvery spikelets on rough stalks; 30–45 cm (1–1½ ft).

E. vaginatum (hare's-tail) grows in tussocks with very narrow leaves and many slender flower spikes each bearing a single, erect, ovoid cluster of dense white, silky hairs about 2.5 cm (1 in) across. Height 25–30 cm (10–12 in).

EICHHORNIA *(Pontederiaceae)*

A handsome genus of tropical S. American aquatics which includes the floating water hyacinth (see p. 102). All possess bright showy flowers in summer, borne on spikes or panicles. Full sunshine is essential and good soil with plenty of space for development. Propagated by cutting off and planting stolons from the parent plant or in some cases seed.

E. azurea (Pontederia azurea) (peacock hyacinth). Suitable only for large pools as the stems creep across the surface of the water up to 1.5–1.8 m (5–6 ft) if the water is warm, although repeated cutting back keeps it in check. The shiny, leathery leaves with spongy petioles vary greatly in size and the funnel-shaped, lavender blue flowers with purple centres and yellow blotches are borne on stout, erect scapes. The six perianth segments of each bloom are united at the base and again at the top, leaving three apertures (or windows, as Seubert calls them in *Flora Braziliensis*), the purpose of which is not quite clear. A possible explanation is that they provide an access for pollinating insects.

E. paniculata (E. martiana) grows about 30 cm (1 ft) above the water and has smooth, shiny, heart-shaped, long-petioled leaves and panicles of 2.5 cm (1 in) wide flowers, the lower petals being rich purple, the three upper ones pale blue with a conspicuous lemon-yellow blotch in the centre of each.

GLYCERIA *(Gramineae)* sweet grass, manna grass

These perennial, waterside grasses are of some importance in parts of Europe for providing grain for wildfowl. *G. fluitans* produces an abundance of seeds which are eaten by geese, ducks and some fish—especially trout—and the grass is greatly relished by horses, cattle and pigs. In parts of Germany and Poland the seeds—known as manna seeds—are also used in soups and gruel. Propagation by seeds and division but in the water garden plants need to be kept under control.

G. maxima (G. aquatica) is an erect grass up to 2 m (6 ft) tall, with large, branched, leafy flower spikes in midsummer. The only kind grown in water gardens is the 45–60 cm (1½–2 ft) *G.m. variegata*, commonly called *G. spectabilis fol. var.* in the trade. This has its leaves regularly striped with green, yellow and white and is herbaceous, the young foliage suffused with rose, which adds to its attraction.

GRATIOLA *(Scrophulariaceae)*

G. officinalis (gratiole). A smooth perennial found in wet European meadows, having serrated, lanceolate leaves and 1½–2 cm (½–¾ in) pinkish-white, or occasionally blue or purple, tubular, axillary flowers. It grows about 30 cm (1 ft) tall and blooms from early summer until autumn. The roots are emetic and the leaves are used for treating bruises. Propagated by division or seed.

HOUTTUYNIA *(Saururaceae)*

H. cordata, a monotypic plant growing 15–37 cm (6–15 in) high with bluish-green cordate leaves, reddish stems and, in late summer, green cone-shaped spikes of flowers each set off by four to six prominent, white, basal bracts. There is a double form 'Flore Pleno' in which the flower centres develop into cones of white petal-like bracts. The leaves have a strong orange smell when bruised, and in sunny situations take on rich autumnal tints. The plant is hardy and will grow in flower borders as well as bog gardens but is invasive so must be kept in check. Propagated by division.

HYDROCERA *(Balsaminaceae)* water balsam

H. triflora is an amphibious plant from Indo-Malaysia with long, ascending or floating branches bearing numerous long fibrous roots when floating. Upright stems carry alternate, up to about 10 cm (4 in), linear leaves, and from mid to late summer large irregular flowers, purplish-red with yellow stamens. In parts of Andhra Pradesh these are used to dye finger-nails. Suitable for warm pools only, the plant is annual but easily reproduced from seed.

HYDROCLEYS *(see* p. 102*)*

HYPERICUM *(Guttiferae)*

H. elodes (marsh St John's wort). A small creeping perennial found growing in bogs and swamps of western Europe, with softly hairy, heart-shaped or rounded leaves half clasping the stems and a few pale yellow flowers, 1½ cm (½ in) across in clusters in late summer. Height 15–23 cm (6–9 in). Useful for masking the edges of artificial pools. Propagated by division.

IRIS *(Iridaceae)*

This well-known family includes a number of plants which appreciate perpetually moist soil, although they object to standing water. These are described on p. 127 but there are also several species which are true aquatics, thriving at the pool margin and flowering freely year after year. All are propagated by division —essential for cultivars—or from seed.

    I. laevigata, Japan and eastern Siberia. One of the best blue-flowered aquatics for early summer, growing 60–75 cm (2–2½ ft) tall with fine strap-shaped leaves and large 10–15 cm (4–6 in) rich blue flowers which have golden claw markings on the falls. It does equally well in shallow water or boggy ground but will not tolerate drought. The species is often confused with the somewhat similar clematis-flowered *I. kaempferi*, also from Japan, a plant which only tolerates standing water in summer. During winter the roots must be kept fairly dry or they will rot. See p. 127. However, it is easy to distinguish between the species by running the fingers up the leaves, for it is possible to feel a prominent midrib in those of *I. kaempferi*, whereas those of *I. laevigata* are smooth throughout.

Forms and cultivars derived from the type include 'Alba', a free-flowering white; 'Atropurpurea', rich violet; 'Colchesteri', white but heavily mottled with deep blue on edges of falls; 'Benikiren', blue-washed and mottled silver; 'Albo Purpurea', white standards, falls purple mottled with white round the edges; 'Variegata', lavender blue with green and cream striped foliage, and 'Rose Queen', a hybrid with *I. kaempferi* having old rose, broad-petalled flowers.

I. pseudacorus (yellow flag), Europe, Asia Minor. Thought to have been the inspiration for the Fleur de Lys of heraldry. The plant will grow in marshy ground or shallow water and has 7–8 cm ($3–3\frac{1}{2}$ in) rich yellow flowers on 60–90 cm (2–3 ft) stems and sword-like leaves. Varieties include 'Bastardii', a softer yellow; 'Golden Queen', larger and more vivid, and 'Variegata', a fine form with gold leaf variegations in spring which disappear in late summer. The acrid roots of the yellow flag were at one time used as a remedy for coughs and toothache, and the roasted seeds as a substitute for coffee.

JUNCUS *(Juncaceae)* rush
In spite of its size this genus, comprising some 300 species, has very few worth growing. The majority are weedy and troublesome to eradicate when once established and even the exceptions should have their roots confined in a planting pocket or be grown in a container.

Yet the family has a long history of economic usage. The pith of some species was employed in medieval England for candlewicks and rush tapers; floors were strewn with rushes before carpets became more plentiful, and the earliest betrothal rings were made from *Juncus communis*. 'Rings of rushes' were mentioned by Shakespeare as well as Spenser—'the knotted Rush-ringes and gilt Rosemarie'. Even today the dried stems are used to make chair seats, baskets and mats.

J. effusus 'Spiralis' (corkscrew rush) is a variant of a cosmopolitan species growing 45 cm ($1\frac{1}{2}$ ft) tall, its round green pithy stems twisted in spiral fashion like a corkscrew. It is propagated by division.

JUSSIAEA *(see* LUDWIGIA*)*

LIMNANTHEMUM *(see* NYMPHOIDES*)*

LIMNOCHARIS *(Butomaceae)*
L. flava (Florida and Louisiana to Brazil and Peru) is a tender plant needing a

temperature of 18°C (65°F) or more for shallow water, and growing 30–60 cm (1–2 ft) high. It is of stoloniferous habit with heart-shaped leaves on long petioles and umbels of yellow, 2–4 cm ($\frac{3}{4}$–$\frac{1}{2}$ in) three-petalled flowers. It flowers in summer and is propagated by division.

LOBELIA *(Lobeliaceae)*
L. paludosa (swamp lobelia), a perennial found in N. American pools growing 30–120 cm (1–4 ft), with flat, oblong leaves 5–10 cm (2–4 in) long, and attractive spikes of 1.2 cm ($\frac{1}{2}$ in) pale blue, tubular flowers in summer. Propagated by division or cuttings.

LUDWIGIA *(Onagraceae)* false loosestrife
Widespread genus of moisture loving plants of the Old and New Worlds, especially in warmer regions. The species can be creeping or erect, mostly having smooth, simple, alternate, 5–12 cm (2–4$\frac{1}{2}$ in) leaves and small, single, axillary or terminal clusters of yellow or white flowers. The aquatic forms are commonly used in aquaria for decorative effects; the large-flowered types as marginals or edgings on wet mud around tropical pools. Propagated by division or cuttings.

    L. alternifolia (rattlebox, seedbox). An erect, rather woody perennial from

Ludwigia × mulertii

the eastern United States, growing to 1 m (3 ft) with solitary, insignificant 1.2 cm (½ in) yellow flowers in the upper leaf axils.

L. clavellina (*Jussiaea repens*). The floating jussiaea has creeping or floating stems 30–90 cm (1–3 ft) in length with small, olive-green, shiny leaves and axillary, inch-wide golden flowers standing above the water. Tropical America.

Var. *grandiflora*, commonly offered by aquatic dealers as *Jussiaea grandiflora*. This frost sensitive aquatic has creeping rhizomes, grows up to 60 cm (2 ft) high and has lanceolate, 2.5–7.5 cm (1–3 in) long, pointed leaves and large, 2.5 cm (1 in) five-petalled, bright yellow flowers. Peru to Carolina.

L. palustris (*Isnardia palustris*) (water purslane), U.S.A. to Costa Rica, W. Indies. Similar to *L. repens* but greener. Stem procumbent or floating, generally branched and rooting at lower nodes. Flowers insignificant.

L. × *mulertii* (*L. repens* × *L. palustris*) is a sterile plant widely grown in the trade and very like *L. repens* in appearance.

L. repens (*L. natans*), U.S.A. and W. Indies. Widely used in aquaria; the leaves bronze-green above, crimson purple under. Small insignificant flowers.

L. suffruticosa (*Jussiaea fruticosa*), S. America. Makes a compact bush, 60–90 cm (2–3 ft) tall, with reddish stems and 7.5–10 cm (3–4 in) lanceolate leaves with small axillary yellow flowers.

LYCOPUS *(Labiatae)* gypsywort, water horehound
L. europaeus, a weedy, European and Asian plant with erect 30–100 cm (1–3 ft) stems, deeply cut lanceolate leaves up to 10 cm (4 in) and axillary whorls of 3 mm (⅛ in) purple dotted, white flowers. The juice of this plant yields a black dye which gypsies once used to dye their skin, the better to pass for Africans by their tanned looks—to muddle the credulous and ignorant by the practice of magic and fortune-telling. Needs shallow water. Propagated by seed and division.

MARSILEA *(Marsileaceae)* pepperwort, water clover
Aquatic ferns from tropical and temperate marshes, with creeping stems and four-parted leaves like four-leaved clovers, each leaflet 1–2 cm (½–¾ in) long. These float in deep water or stand erect 7.5–15 cm (3–6 in) high in shallow. The flowers are insignificant. Grown in indoor or tropical pools or aquaria, or as pot plants in greenhouses.

M. drummondii, Australia; *M. hirsuta*, Australia; and *M. quadrifolia*, Europe and Asia, are hardy in Zone 5; all are very similar.

MENTHA *(Labiatae)* mint
M. aquatica (water mint), Europe. Chiefly noteworthy on account of its aromatic, 2–6 cm (1–2½ in) or more, oval, hairy, toothed leaves and clustered spikes of pale lavender flowers on leafy 30 cm (1 ft) stems in summer. Of creeping habit and readily increased by division.

Menyanthes trifoliata

MENYANTHES *(Menyanthaceae)*

M. trifoliata (bog bean, buck bean), north temperate regions. An aquatic with a horizontal, rhizomatous rootstock, capable of scrambling in and out of water and wet mud, so useful for masking the edges of artificial pools. Foliage trifoliate, like thick $2\frac{1}{2}$–7 cm (1–3 in) bean leaves; flowers borne in early spring on spikes, pink in the bud but opening to $1\frac{1}{2}$ cm ($\frac{1}{2}$ in) fringed white flowers. Height 30 cm (1 ft). The greenish rhizomes have been used medicinally and (instead of hops) in the brewing of beer. Propagated by division.

MICRANTHEMUM *(Scrophulariaceae)*

Small creeping aquatics sometimes grown in aquaria or as marginals to cover wet mud in warm pools.

M. umbrosum (*M. orbiculatum*) from tropical America resembles a miniature creeping Jenny (*Lysimachia nummularia*) with tiny, 0.5 cm ($\frac{1}{4}$ in) round, opposite, green leaves and white two-lipped flowers in summer. Propagated by division.

MONOCHORIA *(Pontederiaceae)*

A genus of rhizomatous plants allied to and resembling *Pontederia cordata*.

M. cyanea and *M. vaginalis*, both from tropical Asia and Australia, are much alike with smooth, long-petioled, cordate or oblong-lanceolate leaves 5–20 cm

(2–8 in) wide, and groups of deep violet-blue flowers 2.5 cm (1 in) wide in racemes. Height 60 cm (2 ft). Suitable for shallow water in warm pools. Summer flowering and propagated by division.

MYOSOTIS *(Boraginaceae)* forget-me-not

M. palustris, Europe. The little water forget-me-not, with its oblong, hairy leaves and bright blue flowers with yellow or pink eyes, is ideal for wet mud or very shallow water. Height 22.5–30 cm (9–12 in). 'Mermaid' is a taller and deeper blue form, 'Semperflorens' dwarfer at 15–20 cm (6–8 in). Propagated from seed.

MYRIOPHYLLUM *(Haloragaceae)* milfoil *(see also* p. 93).

M. proserpinacoides, also known as *M. brasiliense* and *M. aquaticum* (parrot's feather). Brazil, Argentina, naturalized in southern U.S.A. A favourite for trailing over fountain basins or from the margins of raised pools. It is a rampant grower, usually destroyed by frosts, but if cuttings are rooted in late summer and kept in a frost-free place plants can be safely over-wintered. The feathery, finely cut, light green leaves grow in dense whorls round the stems, the tips rising 15–20 cm (6–8 in) out of the water or turning up at the ends. In late summer these tips turn crimson, while the rest of the foliage remains green. Inconspicuous white flowers occur in the leaf axils.

Nymphoides indica

NYMPHOIDES *(Menyanthaceae)* floating heart
A genus of widely distributed, pretty aquatics with floating leaves and flowers just above the surface all summer. They are frequently grown in tubs or small ponds, in loam covered with sand and shallow water. *N. aquatica* is also much used for aquaria. Propagation by division, each section having a flowering joint and leaf.

N. aquatica (*Limnanthemum aquaticum*), southern U.S.A. The banana plant of aquarists, so called because of its clusters of blunt tuberous roots. Leaves round, to 15 cm (6 in) across, violet spotted; flowers white 1.8 cm ($\frac{3}{4}$ in) across.

N. humboldtiana (*Limnanthemum humboldtianum*), tropical America. Fringed white flowers with yellow centres and almost round leaves.

N. indica (*Limnanthemum indicum*) (water snowflake), tropics. A charming little plant with small, round, floating leaves and clusters of dainty, white, fringed flowers with yellowish centres; numerous, lasting one day.

N. peltata (*Limnanthemum peltatum*) (water fringe), Europe, Asia, naturalized in U.S.A. Grows in long trails from which emanate rounded leaves mottled with purple, about 5 cm (2 in) across; large 2.5 cm (1 in) golden yellow, poppy-like flowers in clusters 5–7.5 cm (2–3 in) above the surface. Can be weedy so thin out occasionally. The only species hardy in cold climates.

ORONTIUM *(Araceae)* golden club
O. aquaticum, N. America. A handsome aquatic suitable for deep or shallow water, provided it has full sun. In shallow water it grows 30–45 cm (1–1$\frac{1}{2}$ ft), with aerial oblong-elliptic leaves 12–30 cm (5–12 in) long and 12 cm (5 in) wide, dark velvety green, silvery beneath and coated with a protective wax impervious to water. In deep water the leaves float. Flowers yellow, in late spring and early summer, studding the tops 2–5 cm (1–2 in) of white, pencil-thick 15–60 cm (6–24 in) stems. They then look like golden pokers. Needs deep loamy soil and propagated by division or seeds. The seeds were eaten by Indians as a vegetable, also the roots after their acrid poisonous properties had been removed by roasting.

PELTANDRA *(Araceae)* arrow arum
Hardy, N. American plants for pond margins, producing glossy, arrow-shaped leaves up to 35 cm (14 in) long and 20 cm (8 in) wide, with 7–10 cm (3–4 in) arum-like flowers in mid-spring. Propagated by seeds or division.

P. sagittifolia (*P. alba*) has white flowers followed by red berries.

P. virginica has green flowers with green berries. This species grows to a height of 60 cm (2 ft).

PHILYDRUM *(Philydraceae)*
P. lanuginosum, Australia. A biennial for shallow, warm water pools; short-stemmed with basal, linear leaves and spikes of yellow flowers something like

those of a pea flower. Height 60–90 cm (2–3 ft). More interesting than beautiful. Propagated by seed.

PONTEDERIA *(Pontederiaceae)*

P. cordata. The pickerel weed of N. America, so called from pickerel, a young pike, since these freshwater fish are common in the rivers and streams where the plant grows wild. It is one of the best and easiest marginal aquatics for small, medium or large pools, neat in habit with glossy, heart-shaped leaves atop smooth, rounded 60 cm (2 ft) stems and 15 cm (6 in) spikes of soft blue flowers in late summer. Never invasive, and flowering from summer through autumn when most marginal aquatics are past their best, it should be grown in heavy, fibre-free loam in large pots, aquatic baskets or planting pockets built into the sides of concrete. It should be established in spring, and, when necessary, divided for reproduction purposes at the same season.

Blue-flowered aquatics are rare so this is a plant to treasure. Arrange for it to have 10–15 cm (4–6 in) of water over the crowns and keep the plants towards the sides of the pool. In warmer parts of America the edible seeds have been occasionally eaten, mostly by Indians as a famine food. A form called *angustifolia* (*P. lanceolata*) is taller with linear lanceolate leaves.

POTENTILLA *(Rosaceae)*

P. palustris (Comarum palustre) (marsh cinquefoil, purple marshlocks), Europe, N. America. A low-growing plant of little beauty growing about 30 cm (1 ft) high with strawberry-like, coarsely-toothed leaflets and 3 cm ($1\frac{1}{4}$ in) reddish-purple, five-petalled flowers in summer. Propagated from the stolons.

PRESLIA *(Labiatae)*

P. cervina (Mentha cervina), W. Europe. A smooth, strong-smelling plant related to the mints with small, lance-shaped leaves, shallowly toothed and 30 cm (1 ft) leafy stems carrying a few dense whorls of pinkish-mauve flowers in summer. Needs damp mud or very shallow water. Increased by division.

RANUNCULUS *(Ranunculaceae)* buttercup (*see also* pp. 96 & 138)

R. lingua (spearwort), Europe, temperate Asia. Grows 60–90 cm (2–3 ft) high with lanceolate, ovate leaves up to 20 cm (8 in) long and branching stems carrying many large, bright yellow buttercup-like flowers, 5 cm (2 in) across, through the summer. The form *grandiflora* has larger flowers. Propagated by division.

SAGITTARIA *(Alismataceae)* arrowhead

These are handsome albeit rampant aquatics, some species of which are popular for aquaria (see p. 97). The emergent forms are best planted in 10–15 cm (4–6 in) of water, but some succeed in greater depths. They are reproduced by division of the tubers, which are frequently cultivated in the Orient for their edible quality. The best include:

S. *montevidensis*, warm N. and S. America. The giant arrowhead, which grows to 75 cm (2½ ft) with large, arrow-shaped leaves rarely up to 40 cm (16 in) long and spikes of showy, white, three-petalled flowers 5–7 cm (2–3 in) across which have purple spots at the base. It is not hardy to frost.

S. *sagittifolia* (swamp potato, European arrowhead), has an almost round, small black rhizome, scapes of 2.5 cm (1 in) white flowers on 36–45 cm (15–18 in) stems and three types of leaves: the submerged kinds linear, floating oval and the emergent arrow-shaped.

'Flore Pleno' (S. *japonica* Hort.), with double flowers, looks like a white-flowered stock and is much the most attractive, slow to spread and only needing shallow water.

Sagittaria tubers of one kind or another have been eaten by many people. They are a cultivated vegetable in China and became a favourite food plant of American Indians who knew them as wapatoo. The Indians gathered the crop by wading in the mud where the plants grew and pulled off the tubers with their bare toes.

SAURURUS *(Saururaceae)* lizard's tail
S. *cernuus* (water dragon, swamp lily), N. America. Grows 60–150 cm (2–5 ft) tall from long, aromatic, creeping rhizomes; leaves broadly to narrowly heart-shaped to 15 cm (6 in) long, 5–7 cm (2–3 in) wide. Flowers in 10–15 cm (4–6 in) long, nodding spikes, fragrant, white in summer.

S. *chinensis* (S. *loureirii*), Japan. Strong-smelling with thick rhizomes. Stems 30–45 cm (1–1½ ft), leaves heart-shaped, 10–12 cm (4–5 in) long, flowers yellowish-white.

SCIRPUS *(Cyperaceae)* bulrush
A large, widely distributed and somewhat confused genus of about 200 species found in wet moors, bogs and marshes. Being of stoloniferous habit they can become invasive and only a few varieties can be recommended for ornamental pools. All are propagated by means of division or seed.

S. *lacustris*, Europe, N. America, Asia. Found in flowing rivers. Bears fat, dark green rushes 1–2½ m (3–8 ft) high with bunches of insignificant brown flowers. In early times it was known as pool rush, now corrupted to bulrush, and is still used for making mats, ropes and chair bottoms and for thatching. The pith has been used for paper making.

SCUTELLARIA *(Labiatae)*
S. *galericulata* (skull-cap), Europe, N. America. A widespread plant of temperate regions, growing 30–60 cm (1–2 ft) high, bearing in summer bright blue, snap-dragon-like flowers arranged in remote axillary pairs and oblong 6 cm leaves.

Nelumbo nucifera is the sacred lotus of the Hindoos and carries its large round leaves high above the water. Its poppy-shaped flowers are usually pink.

Caltha palustris. Marsh marigolds are among the earliest aquatics to flower in spring, producing myriads of golden buttercup-like flowers in shallow water or wet mud.

SPARGANIUM *(Sparganiaceae)*
S. erectum (*S. ramosum*) (bur-reed, bede sedge), Europe and N. America. A large aquatic, to 150 cm (5 ft) with linear leaves which are triangular at the base, and branched inflorescences of round spiky flowers and fruits. Wildfowl nest, live and feed on the plant. It is inclined to be rampant so must be kept in check but will grow in running water. Propagated by division.

THALIA *(Marantaceae)*
Tall aquatics for wet soil or shallow water in frost-free regions; or they may be grown in pots which can be lifted and taken under cover for winter. Propagated by division.

T. *dealbata*, warm temperate America. Growing 2–3 m (6–10 ft) high, this species has large, long-petioled, canna-like leaves 50 cm (20 in) long and 25 cm (10 in) wide, and erect branching panicles of small bluish-purple flowers. The plant is covered with white powder which gives it a glaucous appearance.

T. *geniculata* (*T. divaricata*), tropical America, is similar but with zigzag spikes of purple flowers and no white powdering. The leaves are also longer reaching 80 cm (32 in).

TYPHA *(Typhaceae)* reed-mace
Well-known plants with a worldwide distribution. All have creeping rootstocks, flat grassy leaves of varying widths and long, poker-like heads of flowers. All need to have their roots restricted and to be prevented from indiscriminate seeding. Suitable for 2–30 cm (1–12 in) of water, they can be propagated by seed or division.

T. *angustifolia*, Europe, W. Asia, N. America, Australia, N. Africa. A graceful species to 2 m (6 ft), male and female flowers light brown and separated by a plain zone. Leaves about 5 mm ($\frac{1}{2}$ in) across.

T. *latifolia* (common catstail, reedmace), Europe, Asia, N. America. Often erroneously called bulrush, a name correctly belonging to *Scirpus lacustris*. Not generally recommended for ornamental pools and lakes as it is too invasive. Thick poker-heads of flowers. Height 3 m (10 ft). Much used for mats, baskets and the like while floss from the flowers makes a substitute for kapok and down as a filling for cushions and pillows. Leaves 1–2 cm ($\frac{1}{2}$–1 in) across.

T. *minima*, Europe. A dwarf species, 30–60 cm (1–2 ft), suitable for small pools and non-rampant. Spikes 7–12 cm (3–5 in) separated in centre.

TYPHONODORUM *(Araceae)*
T. *lindleyanum*, Madagascar, Mauritius and Zanzibar. A striking plant, arum-like with thick stout stems 1–3 m (3–10 ft) high and 30 cm (1 ft) thick; carrying bright yellow arum flowers up to 60 cm (2 ft) in length and huge arrow-shaped leaves up to 100 cm (40 in) long. Only suitable for tropical pools. The seeds are edible. Propagated by seed or division.

Left: *Scirpus tabernaemontani* 'Zebrinus', middle: *Scirpus tabernaemontani* 'Albescens' (both described on p. 163), right: *Sagittaria sagittifolia*, (described on p. 70).

VERONICA *(Scrophulariaceae)*

V. beccabunga (brooklime), Europe, Asia, N. Africa. A succulent plant suitable for pond edges and hardy, 22–30 cm (9–12 in) high with elliptical, smooth leaves and axillary clusters of small, 7–8 mm ($\frac{1}{3}$ in), bright blue, forget-me-not flowers all summer. Propagated by seed, division or cuttings.

VILLARSIA *(Menyanthaceae)*

Pretty water plants, mostly Australian, for wet soil or very shallow water but not capable of withstanding much frost. Grow at the margins of pools in warm temperate climates or in a covered water garden. All have rounded or oval leaves and yellow flowers and are propagated by division or seed.

V. exaltata (*V. reniformis*), *V. ovata* and *V. parnassifolia* grow 30–60 cm (1–2 ft), 15–30 cm ($\frac{1}{2}$–1 ft), and 30–60 cm (1–2 ft) respectively.

XANTHOSOMA *(Araceae)*

Handsome aroids which can be grown in a pot and stood in a saucer of water or in an indoor pool if temperatures are not high enough for them to be grown outdoors.

X. lindenii (Indian kale, spoon-flower), Colombia. Has a tuberous rootstock with large, arrow-shaped leaves of glossy green up to 45 cm (18 in) long, marked with white alongside the veins and midribs; petioles 1.25 m (4 ft); flowers white, nearly 15 cm (6 in) long.

X. violaceum (blue taro), W. Indies. Has violet leafstalks up to 2 m (6 ft) long and violet margins to the green leaves and yellow flowers in 30 cm (1 ft) spathes. The tubers are edible.

8

Submerged aquatics

Although usually inconspicuous, submerged aquatics are very important plants for the pool, since they provide the key to correct balance, which is the basic secret of clear water.

If we keep fish in a pond they find food in various small creatures which lurk between the vegetation. Plenty of submerged plants ensure shelter for them, and they are thus able to reproduce and maintain the supply. Underwater plants also provide nursery accommodation for fish, which lay their eggs on the leaves and stems, and later these shelter the newly hatched fry from the cannibalistic attentions of their parents. This protective function of the plants is most important.

Again, during the normal growth processes associated with photosynthesis, submerged vegetation returns to the water some of the oxygen lost through respiration of both plants and animals. Carbon dioxide is taken in via the leaves, the chlorophyll in which—with the energy derived from sunlight acting as a source of power—uses the carbon, together with water taken up by the roots, to make simple sugars. This basic form of plant food can be used at once by the plant or stored—for example as starch—in the swollen stem-tubers or roots. Following this operation one chemical element, oxygen, is unneeded so this is returned to the air by free-standing or emergent leaves, or to the water in the case of submerged foliage. Plants which have their leaves continually immersed are therefore known as oxygenating plants and on a sunny day bubbles of oxygen escaping from a plant like *Elodea canadensis* can be seen rising to the surface of the water.

To perform photosynthesis such plants naturally require carbon dioxide and this is provided not only from their own respiratory processes but from fish and other animals, which throughout their lives, day and night, breathe in oxygen and emit carbon dioxide.

Submerged aquatics also play an important part in maintaining water clarity. Their constant demand for food deprives the minute unicellular plants known as algae—chief cause of cloudy water—from light and dissolved salts, both of which are essential to their existence. This particular function is more fully described in Chapter 12, p. 164.

Submerged plants are also aesthetically important to aquarists, for, apart from the uses already mentioned, they furnish attractive backdrops in aquaria. A wide range of leaf shapes, textures and patternings, together with a selection of heights, makes for interesting and colourful backgrounds. Modern aquarists, particularly those who use pumps to augment the supply of oxygen for their fishes, are especially interested in this artistic aspect, and show a tendency to experiment with plants which are not aquatics. Many such are house plants but since aquatic dealers stock them for aquaria and in spite of the fact that they are almost useless as oxygenators and have a restricted life, some people may wish to try out plants like alternantheras, fittonias and ophiopogons.

Among the true submerged aquatics some are more efficient oxygenators than others. A few are very rampant, and can be a real nuisance in a small pool. *Potamogeton natans*, for example, which has floating, oblong, shiny leaves (as well as submerged ones) should never be planted. It is a rampageous pest liable to choke water lilies and other plants and rapidly take possession of most of the water surface. At one time *Elodea canadensis* was invasive in Britain, simply because a very vigorous clone was originally introduced, but through some physiological change most of its vitality ultimately waned and it is no longer a source of trouble to water gardeners.

The planting of submerged water plants can take place at any time during the summer months by the method described on p. 23. They can also be propagated by division or from cuttings taken in spring or summer. Young pieces of new growth should be detached and cut beneath a joint with a sharp knife. The cuttings may then be inserted in shallow pans of sifted loam with a little added charcoal, and submerged in tanks 15–30 cm (6–12 in) deep. They soon root and may then be planted in deeper water if required.

In the list of plants following, 'H' denotes those hardy in pools subject to frost; 'C' denotes plants suitable for cold water aquaria; and 'T' indicates non-hardy plants for warm pools or tropical aquaria.

ALDROVANDA *(Droseraceae)*
A. vesiculosa, Timor, Australia, Europe, S. Africa. A carnivorous plant, rather rare and seldom seen in cultivation but fascinating because it floats without rooting, the stems 5–20 cm (2–8 in) long with close whorls of wedge-shaped, bristly leaves along their length. These are furnished with minute glands which trap small water creatures. Flowers rare, green and white, arranged in fives (sepals, petals, stamens). Needs acid water. T.

AMMANIA *(Lythraceae)*
Small plants with narrowly oblong, opposite leaves, 25–50 mm (1–2 in) long, green to palish red, found in nature in swamps, lakes and ponds. These recently

introduced aquarium plants all have small reddish, axillary flowers and need plenty of light. Those in cultivation include: *A. baccifera* from Asia, *A. senegalensis* from Africa, and *A. verticillata*, Asia. T.

ANUBIAS *(Araceae)*

A small genus, all W. African, with creeping horizontal rhizomes, thick cordate or oval leaves and typical arum flowers. All the species do best in soft water with flowers and leaves partly emerged. Propagated by root division.

A. afzelii (*A. congensis*). Lanceolate leaves, 20 × 10 cm (8 × 4 in), long-petioled, dark green; flower spathes green and fleshy.

A. lanceolata (*A. afzelii* var. *lanceolata*). Leaves narrowly lanceolate, fleshy, long-petioled; flowers greenish-white. Actually a bog plant.

A. nana. Grows 10–20 cm (4–8 in) tall with cordate or ovate leaves; creeping, branching rhizomes; pale green flowers. The best for aquarium work. T.

APONOGETON *(Aponogetonaceae)*

A large family of aquatics, some floating (see p. 52), some submerged; from Asia, Australia, Africa and particularly Madagascar. The African species have forked, twin-spiked flower stems, the others a single spike, most being sweetly scented and bisexual. The submerged kinds, to be grown satisfactorily, must have lime-

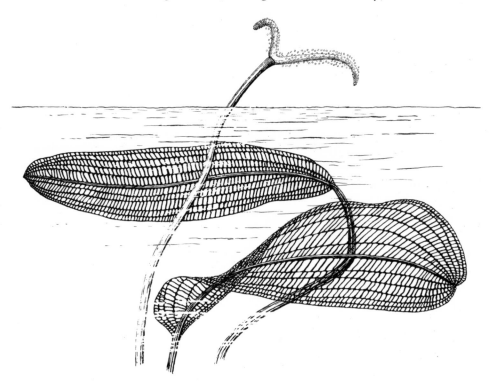

Aponogeton fenestralis

free, slightly acid water. Plant the tuberous rootstocks in equal parts of charcoal, sand and old clay, give good light but not direct sunlight and water temperatures around 18–20°C (64–68°F) which can be reduced to 16–18°C (60–64°F) during the resting period.

The most attractive species are those with open lattice or skeletonized leaves like *A. fenestralis* (*Ouvirandra fenestralis*), *A. henkelianus*, and to a lesser extent *A. bernerianus*, all from Madagascar. These have tuberous roots, olive green oblong leaves up to 10 or 20 cm (4–8 in) long and 25–75 mm (1–3 in) wide, which are mere traceries of nerves and cross veins, so have a delicate, lacy appearance. Occasionally some leaves are wholly or partly filled in with green tissue. Twin spikes of white or pinkish flowers. All need shade or shelter from strong light.

A. crispus from Ceylon, also tuberous-rooted, bears long, narrow, bright to dark green, long-stemmed, solid leaves up to 30 cm (1 ft) long with crisped edges and a single, 15 cm (6 in) long spike of white or cream flowers above the water.

Similar but with still more crisped leaf edges are the Australian yellow-flowered *A. elongatus*; *A. undulatus* from India and Ceylon, white-flowered and hardier than most with some floating leaves; and *A. ulvaceus*, a yellowish, twin flower-spiked, Madagascan species with translucent leaves. The latter tolerates lime in the water and seeds freely in cultivation. Other species occasionally available are *A. boivinianus* from Madagascar with white twin spikes; *A. longiplumolosus*, a newly discovered Madagascan species with twin or triple, pale violet flower spikes; *A. loriae*, a green-flowered, lime tolerant kind native to Australia; and *A. natans* with white flowers from Ceylon. T.

BACOPA *(Scrophulariaceae)*
B. amplexicaulis (*Herpestis amplexicaulis, Septilia caroliniana, B. caroliniana, Monniera amplexicaulis*) water hyssop. A bog plant from south and central U.S.A. growing up to 60 cm (2 ft) with sturdy, rounded stems thickly clothed with 20 mm ($\frac{3}{4}$ in) long and 10 mm ($\frac{3}{8}$ in) wide, fleshy, opposite, oval or rounded, stalkless leaves. Grown in shallow water, the plant produces blue, tubular flowers in summer. T.

B. monnieri, cosmopolitan, often found in tropical rice fields. Leaves smaller than preceding and hairless; flowers white or blue. Similar cultivation. T.

BARCLAYA *(Nymphaeaceae)*
B. longifolia. Recently introduced species from Thailand, closely related to nymphaea and found in sluggish forest rivers. Narrow tuberous rootstock with long, narrow, red and green, submerged leaves prominently, veined in red and brown, up to 30 cm (1 ft) long and 3–4 cm (1–2 in) wide. Flowers greenish externally, purplish-red inside, the petals standing on top of the ovary (not below as in nymphaea). They are about 2 cm (1 in) in length and the seeds ripen

below the water. Needs a temperature of 22°C (72°F) or over. Propagated by seed. T.

BLYXA *(Hydrocharitaceae)*

Plants from the warmer regions of Asia and Africa, where they are found in irrigation ditches and rice fields, which have been introduced to N. America where they grow in southern pools. The plants form rosettes of thin, grassy leaves with acute tips, of various lengths 30–90 cm (1–3 ft), according to the depth of water. Flowers on long stems, two-petalled, green and white with three stamens. *B. echinosperma* from India, China and Japan is annual and needs tropical aquarium conditions and temperatures around 25–29°C (77–84°F). Propagated by seed. T.

BOLBITIS *(Lomariopsidaceae)*

Tropical water ferns which will grow in warm water aquaria in temperatures around 22–28°C (72–80°F). They are usually attached to stone and appreciate moving water, so can be placed near filters.

B. heudelotii, tropical Africa. Pinnate incised leaves up to 35 cm (14 in) in length, variously coloured in shades of green and brown.

B. fluviatilis from W. Africa and *B. hydrophylla* from the Philippines are other aquatic species. All grow on rocks and trees by streams. Propagated by careful division. T.

CABOMBA *(Nymphaeaceae)* fanwort, Washington grass

Plants for warm water aquaria or tropical pools with deeply divided, fan-shaped, submerged leaves and round floating leaves. All are easily propagated from cuttings and need lime-free water with temperatures around 18–22°C (64–72°F). T.

Available species include *C. aquatica* from S. America with yellow flowers just above the water; *C. australis*, Brazil, also yellow; *C. caroliniana*, U.S.A., white flowers with yellow spots at petal bases and *C. pulcherrima* (*C. caroliniana* var. *pulcherrima*), U.S.A., reddish flowers.

CALLITRICHE *(Callitrichaceae)* water starwort

Good oxygenators for cold water aquaria and outdoor pools in northern Europe, also areas with similar conditions. They have long, thin, branching stems with small, light green, linear 1–2 cm ($\frac{3}{8}$–$\frac{3}{4}$ in) leaves which bunch at the surface in summer to form starry masses and are often eaten by fish. Fast growing. Flowers insignificant. Propagated by division. H.

Species found in Europe include *C. hermaphroditica* (*C. autumnalis*), always submerged with very fine foliage in late summer; *C. hamulata*, with floating leaves in autumn; *C. palustris* (*C. verna*), at its best in spring and summer; and *C. stagnalis*, a very variable species, usually without floating leaves. H.

CARDAMINE *(Cruciferae)*
C. lyrata (bitter cress), Japan, Korea. A bog plant often used by aquarists for warm water aquaria. It is a dainty little plant with fragile, very thin, bright green, round to heart-shaped leaves occurring in bunches with long, white, trailing roots. White flowers 5–10 mm ($\frac{1}{5}$–$\frac{2}{5}$ in) in diameter occur in clusters. In aquaria it should be grown in sand; temperatures 15–20°C (59–68°F). T.

CERATOPHYLLUM *(Ceratophyllaceae)* hornwort
An exceptionally hardy genus, capable of growing in very deep water (according to Agnes Arber in *Water Plants*), up to 10 m (30 ft) and also under very cold conditions. The bristly, dark green, narrow leaves grow in whorls around the stems and are very brittle. The much-branched stems sometimes reach great lengths to 1–2 m (3–6 ft) but are easily broken with rough handling. The cosmopolitan *C. demersum* and European *C. submersum* are very similar. H.

CHARA *(Characeae)* stonewort
A large genus represented in many parts of the world although only a few are available from dealers. They are rough to the touch, with bristly stems and 2.5 cm (1 in) leaves in whorls on much-branched stems approximately 15–20 cm (6–8 in) in length. Charas (classified by botanists as algae) have the ability to extract lime from water, hence their common name; fossilized seeds and stems have been repeatedly found in limestone formations. They are not particularly good oxygenators, but spread rapidly and shelter small insects though they have an unpleasant smell when handled. The following are cultivated: *C. aspera*, *C. globularis* (*C. fragilis*) and *C. vulgaris* (*C. foetida*). Propagated by division. H.

CRASSULA *(Crassulaceae)*
C. recurva (*Tillaea recurva*), Australia. A creeping plant which grows equally well at the pond edge or submerged in shallow water. It has succulent, fleshy, very fine leaves only 4 mm ($\frac{1}{7}$ in) long and $\frac{1}{2}$ mm ($\frac{1}{50}$ in) wide with minute white flowers. Propagated by division. H.

CRINUM *(Amaryllidaceae)*
C. natans from tropical Africa is a true aquatic bulb. It grows submerged, the long, strap-shaped leaves—which may be up to 1 m ($3\frac{1}{4}$ ft) in length—floating on the water. The flowers are borne in umbels of four to six above the surface, and are white tinged with purple, with purple anthers. It is a rare plant in the aquarium trade but occasionally offered. Propagated by offsets. T.

CRYPTOCORYNE *(Araceae)* water trumpet
Bog plants from the Old World tropics, popular and used in warm water aquaria since 1906. They are slow growing, with very persistent leathery leaves which do not demand high illumination in aquaria but in warm pools where

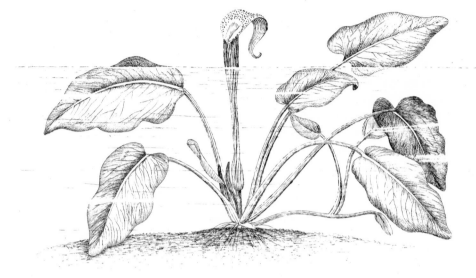

Cryptocoryne griffithii

there is shallow water and more light, producing arum-shaped flowers of various colours and dimensions—fat, thin, spirally twisted, long or squat. They need temperatures of 20–30°C (68–86°F) and soft water which is slightly acid. In aquaria they are usually grown in river sand mixed with peat, or loam. Normally they are propagated by division. There are 50 species of which 14 or 15 are stocked by specialist dealers, some more readily available than others. Keen aquarists collect them like stamps. T.

C. beckettii, reddish-brown foliage 15–25 cm (6–10 in) long, which becomes green when submerged, and purplish flowers; *C. affinis*, leaves dark velvety green, wavy margins, 15–30 cm (6–12 in) long, flowers purple and green; *C. ciliata*, thick, lanceolate, 0.5–1 m ($1\frac{1}{2}$–3 ft) long, bright green leaves, 30 cm (1 ft) tall flowers, purple with yellow spots; *C. griffithii*, 15 cm (6 in) elliptic leaves, long-petioled, dark green above, grey-green beneath, flowers red with yellow throats; *C. lutea* (*C. walkeri*), lanceolate leaves, 10–20 cm (4–8 in) long, oval, flowers greenish-yellow; *C. nevillii*, 5–10 cm (2–4 in) long, narrowly ovate to oblong leaves with tapering points, flowers purplish; *C. wendtii*, brownish to reddish green, 15–20 cm (6–8 in) long leaves with darker vein stripes, elongated, lanceolate, flowers purple with white warts, quick growing; *C. willisii* (*C. axelrodii*), leaves olive green suffused with purple, 25 cm (10 in) long, wavy-margined, flowers greenish-yellow. Others in cultivation include C.

petchii, brownish-green; *C. legroi*, yellow-green; *C. parva*, violet and brown; *C. thwaitesii*, green, red and violet: all from Sri Lanka.

ECHINODORUS *(Alismataceae)*

A popular family of bog and water plants (see baldellia) closely related to sagittarias and mostly from N. and S. America. The flowers have three green sepals, three white petals and from 6 to 50 stamens, although the blooms do not develop under aquarium conditions. The two sexes occur in the same flower giving rise to ball-shaped fruits. All have tuberous rootstocks and both submerged and emergent foliage, although for aquarium work the latter is not encouraged and can be prevented by confining the roots in small pots or constant removal of any leaves which tend to grow upwards.

The leaves grow in rosettes and are usually ribbon-like at first, then broadly heart-shaped or narrowly lanceolate on long petioles. The veining is very prominent, longitudinal with a network of crossing veins. Plants need a winter resting period—when conditions can be cooler—but normally do well in temperatures around 18–24°C (64–75°F), in slightly acid water with good light. Propagated from small plantlets which grow on runners from the parent plant. C and T.

E. amazonicus (*E. brevipedicellatus*), S. America, is popular as it never produces floating leaves. Foliage 25–50 cm (10–20 in) long, strap-shaped, in rosettes with young plants emanating from the base. T. aquaria.

E. angustifolius, a new introduction from Brazil with very narrow, 10 mm ($\frac{2}{5}$ in) leaves. T.

E. argentinensis from S. America has both broad and narrow leaved forms and will grow in either cold or warm water aquaria.

E. berteroi (*E. rostratus*) (cellophane plant). Central America and W. Indies. Leaves narrow and grassy at first, then wider with a heart-shaped base 10–12 cm (4–5 in) long and 8–9 cm (3–3$\frac{1}{2}$ in) wide and finally floating with oval heart-shaped leaves and rounded, arrow-shaped bases. Popular in Europe for cold water aquaria.

E. bleheri (*E. paniculatus*) (Amazon sword plant). An attractive S. American species, very popular for aquaria, with broad, strap-like, bright green leaves 25–45 cm (10–18 in) long on three-edged, narrow stalks. T. Often confused with *E. amazonicus*.

E. cordifolius, U.S.A. Leaves up to 60 cm (2 ft) with heart-shaped blades on long stems which in pools rise above the water. Flowers in whorls on 90 cm (3 ft) stems. C.

E. horemanii, Brazil. Large submerged leaves, 30–50 cm (12–20 in) long, olive green with wavy margins. T.

E. horizontalis (*E. guyanensis*, *E. tunicatus*). Heart-shaped, dark green leaves with sharp points, 40–55 cm (16–22 in) long, also with white flowers which set viable seed. T.

E. latifolius (*E. magdalensis*) (dwarf Amazon sword plant), tropical America. A marsh plant with rosettes of narrow, bright green, lanceolate leaves with dark veins. T. Aquaria.

E. macrophyllus, Brazil, white or yellow flowers and triangular, cordate emergent leaves, the submerged leaves often spotted with red. T.

E. osiris from Brazil has leaves which are frequently reddish. T.

E. tenellus (pygmy-chain sword plant), N. to S. America. Small with narrow, lanceolate leaves to 10 cm (4 in) and about 2 mm ($\frac{1}{12}$ in) wide. A good carpeter, increasing by means of runners in the sandy bottoms of cold water aquaria. Dr. de Wit mentions several forms of this species.

Other echinodorus species occasionally available are: *E. longistylis*, *E. major* (*E. martii*), *E. opacus* and *E. nymphaeifolius*. H and T.

EGERIA (Hydrocharitaceae)

E. densa, S. America. An excellent oxygenator for cold water aquaria as well as outdoor pools in temperate Europe and southern U.S.A. Known erroneously in the trade as *Elodea densa*. It differs from true elodeas in having several white, three-petalled flowers (elodea has only one), produced above the water level and containing nectar. They are also insect-pollinated. True elodeas bear inconspicuous flowers and are fertilized under water. Under favourable condi-

Egeria densa

tions it has branching stems of several feet with whorls of dark green, narrow, linear leaves about 2–3 cm (1 in) long. Propagated by cuttings. C and T.

ELATINE *(Elatinaceae)* waterwort
Small creeping aquatics, frequently branched and rooting at the nodes. Leaves small, spoon-shaped, bright green, fragile, usually continuing to grow in winter. Flowers insignificant. Hardy in Britain, southern Europe and southern U.S.A. Ideal for cold water aquaria as well as pools and propagated by division or cuttings.

   E. americana is the commonest species of America where it is known as the mud purslane; the European (including British) *E. hydropiper* and its form *submersa* are both good ground cover plants and *E. macropoda*, also European, is a well known carpeter with rich green foliage. H.

ELEOCHARIS *(Cyperaceae)* spike rush
E. acicularis (hair grass). A widespread plant of wet ground or shallow water, found in Europe, Asia and N. America. In aquaria it forms tufts of rush-like leaves 5–30 cm (2–12 in) long according to the depth of water, with brown terminal flower spikelets in summer and autumn. H.

   E. dulcis is the Chinese water chestnut, so called because it is cultivated like rice in Asia, in flooded fields, for the sake of its scrunchy white tubers. These can be cooked or eaten raw. The cylindrical stems grow 30–90 cm (1–3 ft) tall and have 5 cm (2 in) flower spikelets. Native to tropical Asia as well as the Pacific Islands and W. Africa. Propagated by division of the tubers. T.

ELISMA *(see* LURONIUM*)*

ELODEA *(Hydrocharitaceae)*
Elodeas are among the best oxygenators for pools or aquaria, forming dense masses of foliage which all day long release bubbles of oxygen to the water. They also shelter fish fry and the small water creatures so esteemed by fish. Usually the foliage grows in whorls around branching stems, each leaf long and narrow or slightly egg-shaped, dark green with a pointed tip. The flowers are insignificant. Elodeas need plenty of light and favour alkaline conditions. Dealers commonly class two species as elodeas which in fact belong to other genera, a mistake repeated year after year. Accordingly water gardeners looking for *Elodea densa* should refer to *Egeria densa* and for *Elodea crispa* to *Lagarosiphon major*. Plants are readily reproduced from the tips of young growing shoots, taken about 7–10 cm (3–4 in) long and replanted.

   E. callitrichoides (Anacharis callitrichoides) (Chilean water weed), Argentina, Chile. A rapid grower producing dense masses of pea-green, linear leaves about 2.5 cm (1 in) long in whorls of three. Can only be grown outside in areas subject to light frosts or in an unshaded aquarium; temperature 10–21°C (50–70°F). H.

E. canadensis (Anacharis canadensis, A. alsinastrum, Philotria canadensis) (Canadian pondweed, water thyme, ditchmoss, Canadian water pest, Babington's curse), N. America but now established in Europe, Australia and parts of Africa and Asia. A hardy species, very vigorous and often found in pools, lakes and other areas of still water, although its numbers fluctuate with growth most prolific in alkaline water. The brittle, branching stems are rather fragile but carry close whorls of leaves, usually in threes. H.

Similar species from N. America introduced to Europe and occasionally grown in unheated aquaria are *E. nuttallii (E. occidentalis)* and *E. longivaginata.*

FONTINALIS *(Fontinalaceae)* incombustible water moss
F. antipyretica, Europe, N. America, N.E. Asia. Water mosses are usually found in cold running water, attached to stones or the wooden struts of old bridges. They are variable plants with many forms, very hardy and invaluable in unheated aquaria or outdoor pools. The species received its specific name because it was at one time used by Swedes to fill the spaces between chimneys and walls and thus, by excluding air, preventing fire. If found in the wild it is best to transfer it with its anchorage if possible, rinsing it under a cold tap to remove unwanted pests. When this is not practical, each slender stem must be attached with thread to portions of old brick, decaying wood or rough stone. The (usually) very dark green, narrow leaves have no midrib but closely clothe the branching stems. Yellow-green or coppery-brown forms are known. If the water gets too warm it will die. Propagate by careful division.

HETERANTHERA *(Pontederiaceae)* mud plantain
Aquatic plants from subtropical and tropical Africa and America, mainly grown in aquaria, but occasionally in indoor or tropical pools. The leaves are of two types—linear when submerged or orbicular when floating; the flowers are regular with six perianth segments, one or several together. Propagation by division or by rooting slips in warmth.

H. dubia (water star grass). A trailing, submerged water plant, the stems up to 1 m (3¼ ft) long, rooting at the nodes. Leaves sessile and linear, up to 15 cm (6 in) long with light yellow flowers just above the water. Favours alkaline water and withstands temperatures down to 10°C (50°F).

H. limosa, N. America. A plant with short, erect, lanceolate to round, radical leaves which become elongated and float in deep water. In shallow water it stands 15–38 cm (6–15 in) above the surface and has single, tubular, blue or white flowers.

H. reniformis has both submerged and floating leaves, the latter kidney- to heart-shaped with glossy surfaces and pale blue flowers, 4–8 to a spike.

H. zosterifolia (H. zosteraefolia), from Brazil, has creeping stems which root at the nodes and up to 5 cm (2 in), sessile, linear, submerged leaves and spoon-shaped floating leaves. The bright blue flowers frequently appear in pairs above the water.

Hottonia palustris

HOTTONIA *(Primulaceae)* water violet, water feather, featherfoil, water yarrow

H. palustris, Europe (including Britain) and W. Asia. One of two species of charming aquatics for shallow water in garden pools or temporary planting in unheated aquaria. It floats just under the water, the branched stems carrying alternate, pinnately divided leaves with long white roots from their nodes. In spring whorls of pale purple flowers are carried on slender stems well above the water—looking something like small *Primula malacoides*. In autumn the plant forms winter buds and disappears until spring.

    H. inflata, S.E. North America, is less attractive, but later blooming with smaller, whitish flowers. The flower stems are swollen, much thickened and spongy, thickly packed with finely divided foliage. Hottonias are propagated by rooting side shoots or from the winter buds. C.

HYDRILLA *(Hydrocharitaceae)*

H. verticillata, N.E. Europe, S.E. Asia, Australia, Madagascar. A plant closely related and very similar to elodea. The green leaves, each about 2 cm ($\frac{3}{4}$ in) long, have toothed margins and grow in whorls of 4–8 up the branching stems. Easily propagated from cuttings. T. C.

HYDROTRICHE *(Scrophulariaceae)*

H. hottoniiflora, the only species in the genus, is a fairly new introduction from Madagascar. It is of creeping habit with whorls of narrow, bright green leaves on the branched underwater stems. These bear close resemblance to cabomba. The white and yellow flowers are held above the water in summer. Propagate by division. T.

HYGROPHILA *(Acanthaceae)*

Tropical marsh plants, some cultivated as aquarium furnishings. The leaves are normally opposite but very varied in the species, sometimes entire, sometimes deeply cut, although usually more or less hairy. The flowers occur in the leaf axils. Propagated from cuttings or occasionally single leaves, which, when detached and pushed into soil, form roots and shoots—like African violets.

    H. angustifolia, India, Ceylon, S. China, has long, narrow, willow-like leaves up to 15 cm (6 in), bright green with pale undersides. Flowers bright purple. T.

    H. difformis (*Synnema triflora*) (water wistaria). A small plant found in India and Thailand and often used submerged in tropical aquaria. The submerged, stalkless, opposite leaves are pinnately divided, the emergent ones lanceolate to oval and darker green than the submerged. Clusters of mauve, violet-streaked flowers occur in the leaf axils. T.

    H. guyanensis, Guyana. Lanceolate leaves, small whitish flowers. T.

    H. polysperma, Bangladesh and Thailand. A popular plant in Asia although only recently introduced to Europe. Of creeping habit with oblong, bright

Iris laevigata 'Variegata'. The variegated leaves of this blue-flowered iris provide an attractive foil to the many shades of green in the garden.

Orontium aquaticum. The bluish-green leaves of the golden club are water repellent and the flowers resemble gold-tipped pokers.

green leaves, which become narrower towards the tops of the stems. Small white or bluish flowers, but rarely seen. T.

H. stricta (*Nomaphila stricta*), Malaya, India. A much-branched plant with oblong or linear lanceolate leaves. Blue, violet and white flowers are produced when plants are grown in wet mud rather than submerged. T.

LAGAROSIPHON *(Hydrocharitaceae)*

L. major (*L. muscoides* var. *major*; *Elodea crispa*). Often but erroneously sold as 'Elodea crispa', this South African native is one of the best oxygenators for small, medium and large pools. It is a soft-stemmed, branching plant heavily clothed with brittle, narrow, curled leaves. The flowers are insignificant and the roots almost non-existent. It is hardy in Britain but will not withstand exceptionally cold winters. C.

LAGENANDRA *(Araceae)*

Asiatic bog plants, similar and closely related to Cryptocoryne (see p. 81). They have simple leaves, mostly elliptic to lanceolate on long petioles, and arum-like flowers, usually purple. Fairly new for aquarium culture, the following species are now making their way into growers' lists.

L. dalzellii (*L. meeboldii*), a small plant 5–10 cm (2–4 in) tall, leaves bronze

Lagarosiphon major

red or green; L. *thwaitesii*, 15 cm (6 in) long leaves with silvery white margin and flecks.

L. *koenigii*, narrow leaves 10–20 mm ($\frac{3}{8}$–$\frac{3}{4}$ in) long. All need temperatures around 22°C (72°F). Propagated by division of the rhizomes.

L. *lancifolia* with 10 cm (4 in) leaves; L. *ovata*, leaves 45 cm (18 in) long and nearly 12.5 cm (5 in) wide.

LIMNOPHILA *(Scrophulariaceae)*

A confused genus since many of the species sold for aquaria do not flower and accordingly cannot always be accurately identified. Aquarists value several for their foliage; those included here are offered by dealers under the following names. Temperatures around 21°C (70°F), good light and a rich growing medium are essential for successful cultivation. Propagate from cuttings or runners. T.

L. *heterophylla* (*Ambulia heterophylla*), India, China, Japan, Ceylon. Produces close whorls of finely cut underwater leaves like those of cabomba (p. 80), and undivided, toothed floating leaves resembling those of the water crowfoot (*Ranunculus aquatilis*). This one does flower, the white blooms having purple stripes in the throat.

L. *indica*. Tropical Asia, Africa, Australia. Very similar to preceding with long white roots emanating from the leaf joints. Stem sap toxic to some fishes and smelling of turpentine. Flowers tubular, pale purple.

L. *sessiliflora* (*Ambulia sessiliflora*), Tropical Asia. Is a beautiful shade of vivid, bright green and bears whorls of finely cut underwater leaves and ranunculus-like floating foliage. Bluish-white flowers occur in the leaf axils.

LITTORELLA *(Plantaginaceae)*

L. *uniflora* (shoreweed), Europe. Produces tufts of rounded, bright green, upright, narrow leaves 5–10 cm (2–4 in) high in rosettes and solitary, staminate flowers with very long filaments. The female flowers are sessile and found amongst the leaves at the base of the male blossoms. Sometimes used in aquaria. Propagated by division. C.

LOBELIA *(Campanulaceae)*

L. *dortmanna* (water lobelia), Europe, N. America. A beautiful plant for cold, clear, acid water usually found in deep northern lakes entirely submerged, or occasionally in wet, sandy soil. It is evergreen, with tufts of stiff, dark green leaves, frequently arched at the tip, 10 cm (4 in) long and 4–5 mm ($\frac{1}{5}$ in) wide with longitudinal veins. Small, bell-shaped, light blue flowers with white bands are carried in loose racemes above the water surface. Propagated by division of the offshoots. H.

LUDWIGIA *(see* p. 64)

LURONIUM *(Alismataceae)*

L. natans (*Alisma natans*, *Elisma natans*) (floating water plantain), Europe. A dainty aquatic, rosette forming, with two kinds of leaves; ribbon-like when submerged, small and egg-shaped when floating; delicate white, three-petalled flowers float on the surface. An ideal plant for shallow rock pools or containers, remaining green all winter. Propagated by division. C.

LYSIMACHIA *(Primulaceae)*

Although not true submerged aquatics, several species are frequently used as such in cold water aquaria. They must have a fair amount of light however or the leaves drop off or lose their colour. The species mentioned may also be planted in wet mud at pond margins.

   L. nummularia (creeping Jenny, moneywort), Europe, eastern U.S.A. A creeping plant with oval-oblong, opposite leaves and under bog conditions showy, five-petalled, bright yellow flowers. There is a golden leaved form. Propagated by division. C.

MYRIOPHYLLUM *(Haloragaceae)* water milfoil, featherfoil

This genus comprises a group of marsh and aquatic plants of great value, for they are attractive to look at, make excellent hosts for fish eggs and are reasonably efficient oxygenators. Propagation is easily effected by breaking off small slips and pushing them into the aquarium or pond compost. They grow in warm or cold, still or running water but need plenty of light. The plants are glabrous, the leaves alternate or opposite, the aquatic kinds usually arranged in whorls and pinnately divided into fine segments. The flowers may be axillary, solitary or spiked; they are very small and insignificant and monoecious (pistil and stamens in separate flowers on the same plant) but flowers are not produced in aquaria—only in pools. They are prone to algae unless aquaria, sand and glass are kept clean. Recommended species for outdoor pools include: *M. alterniflorum*, which has verticillate leaves, three or four in a whorl, stems long, sparsely branched and often free of leaves at the base; *M. heterophyllum* from N. America, naturalized in Europe with leaves in whorls; *M. spicatum*, again with leaves in whorls of four and deciduous in winter; and *M. verticillatum*, a stouter plant with stems up to 2 m ($6\frac{1}{2}$ ft) long bearing crowded whorls of leaves cut into thread-like segments. All are European and hardy in Britain; *M. verticillatum* prefers acid water and *M. spicatum* alkaline.

   Species for warmer water or heated aquaria are: *M. pinnatum* (*M. scabratum*) from southern U.S.A., which has reddish-bronze, narrowly segmented leaves below water and flat, linear ones above; *M. hippuroides* (red water milfiol), from Mexico and southern U.S.A., with reddish, needle-fine leaves; and *M. elatinoides*, a widespread species from Mexico and western N. America to Brazil, Falkland Islands, New Zealand and Tasmania, with blue-green leaves in whorls of four.

M. oguraense and *M. ussuriense* are Japanese, the latter the hardiest and according to Dr de Wit able to tolerate a thin layer of ice on an indoor pool. Both species are green and need to be kept cut back in aquaria or they drop their lower leaves.

NAJAS *(Najadaceae)* bushy pondweed
Slender, branched, extremely brittle, wholly submerged aquatics with fibrous roots. They prefer clear acid water and can be annual or perennial. The annuals are propagated from seed, the perennials from cuttings.

N. flexilis, a European annual with slender, extremely narrow curled leaves of a light translucent green shade. H.

N. graminea, Europe, N. Africa and tropical Asia. An annual in cool waters, perennial in warm. Much branched, 30–46 cm ($1-1\frac{1}{2}$ ft) stems with opposite, fine, linear leaves. H and C.

N. minor, central and southern Europe, annual with forked branches and toothed, sickle-shaped leaves which are very narrow and brittle. H.

N. microdon (*N. guadelopensis*), an American perennial with transparent, olive-green leaves in tufts. H.

NITELLA *(Characeae)*
Like chara, a very old genus of primitive, flowerless plants, related to although not true ferns. They lack true roots, but are valuable for carpeting aquaria and are increased from spores or cuttings. The following species, all European, and most of them cosmopolitan, are occasionally available from dealers: *N. flexilis*, *N. gracilis*, *N. opaca* and *N. capillaris*, all with finely cut, leaf-like phyllodes. H.

NOMAPHILA *(see* HYGROPHILA)

OTTELIA *(Hydrocharitaceae)*
O. alismoides, from tropical and subtropical Asia and originally named *Stratiotes alismoides* by Linnaeus, is a striking, submerged water plant with two kinds of leaves. The young ones are strap-shaped with short petioles, the older leaves long-petioled with broad heart-shaped blades up to 13 cm (5 in) in length and as much across. These are very fragile and easily broken. Small, three-petalled, white or greenish flowers, with smaller bag-like bracts below them, float on the surface. These set seed—the usual method of propagation. Ottelias need slightly acid water and temperatures of 18°C (64°F) or above. In Italy they are often found in rice-fields, but also make attractive aquarium plants. There is another species *O. ulvaefolia*, found in Zimbabwe, which has reddish leaves and yellow flowers. T.

PILULARIA *(Marsileaceae)* pillwort, pepper-grass
P. globulifera. A small European plant of creeping habit with bundles of smooth,

awl-shaped leaves, found near the margins of lakes and pools or occasionally entirely submerged. The pointed leaves, 2.5–10 cm (1–4 in) long are curled when young like the fronds of a fern but assume an erect position when mature. Fructification reveals round spore cases, resembling small peas arising near the bases of the leaves. These split when ripe into quarters, which remain attached to the plant while the spores are scattered. Plants rarely fruit when entirely submerged but when well grown make a pretty green mat. C.

POTAMOGETON *(Potamogetonaceae)* pondweed

A large genus of a 100 or more submerged aquatics found in temperate or (occasionally) tropical regions. The majority are weedy and grow so rapidly that they can destroy choicer and more fragile plants, although a few are suitable for aquaria and pools. In many of the species there are two types of leaves: the submerged ones narrow and often translucent; and broad, floating leaves. In still pools these often present a dirty appearance, due to silt stirred up by fish or layers of calcium carbonate taken from the water settling on the leaves. *P. lucens* produces lime deposits within the cell membranes in similar fashion to chara and nitella, which thus give the leaves greater strength to resist the forces of moving water such as in a stream. *P. natans* roots are said to be appreciated by swans, and ducks will eat the seeds and leaves of *P. crispus* and *P. densus* and so spread the species from one watercourse to another. Most of the genus are very brittle, pellucid and smooth and appear to grow best in clay soils. They also hybridize freely, which makes difficulties over identification. Few are useful for aquaria but several are fair oxygenators for small pools.

P. crispus (curled pondweed), cosmopolitan distribution. Linear oblong, wavy-edged, tapering, almost translucent, alternate, reddish leaves and in summer short spikes of brownish flowers. The plant produces winter buds. H.

P. densus (now more correctly *Groenlandia densa*) (frog's lettuce), Europe. Very like *P. crispus* but without wavy margins to the leaves. H.

P. lucens (shining pondweed), Europe, Asia, Australia, Africa. Has a creeping rhizome, short-stalked, large, glossy, elliptical leaves tapering at both ends on stems which can be several metres in length. The many-flowered inflorescence is a thick spike about 2.5–6 cm (1–2½ in) long. H.

P. natans, the commonest European pondweed, with floating oblong leaves resembling those of the water hawthorn (*Aponogeton distachyus*) but extremely rampant and not recommended for pools. H.

P. pectinatus (fennel-leaved pondweed), Europe, Australia. Much branched, slender stems with thread-like leaves, occurring in both still and running water. H.

P. perfoliatus, cosmopolitan in temperate regions. Leaves oval and alternate, devoid of stalks and tightly clasping the stems. Often bronzed with rough margins. Likes alkaline conditions. H.

Other species are offered by aquatic dealers for tropical aquaria like *P. gayi* from Brazil and Chile with linear leaves on richly branched, brown-green stems.

P. *coloratus* from N. Africa, the Bahamas, Australia and parts of Europe, with reddish, lanceolate-oval leaves; and P. *octandrus* from Old World tropics, with linear submerged leaves and elliptical floating leaves. T.

All potamogetons can be propagated by division.

PROSERPINACA *(Haloragaceae)* mermaid weed
P. *palustris*, West Indies, Brazil and Canada. An attractive swamp plant with strong stems, the submerged leaves of which are very finely cut and arranged in whorls so that they look something like myriophyllum, and nettle-shaped, floating or emergent leaves with toothed margins. Small greenish-white flowers are borne in the axils of the upper leaves. Propagated by division. C.

RANUNCULUS *(Ranunculaceae)*
R. *aquatilis* (water crowfoot). Europe, N. America. One of the few non-poisonous members of the buttercup family; horses, hogs and cows all feed on it when provided as fodder. It is also a good oxygenator and small slips broken off will root in aquaria, although it does best in stagnant ponds or lakes, also in slow-running water, where it often forms large colonies, spangling the water in spring with myriads of snow-white, five petalled, yellow-based flowers.

Ranunculus aquitilis

There are two kinds of leaves, the lower ones submerged and finely dissected into numerous segments, the upper leaves kidney-shaped, mostly three-lobed and floating.

R. circinatus (*R. divaricatus*) (rigid-leaved crowfoot), Europe, N. Africa. Has no floating leaves, only submerged leaves divided into very narrow, stiff segments, almost round in shape. These come on very long, leafy stems. Unlike *R. aquatilis*, these do not collapse when taken out of the water. The white flowers, 1–2 cm ($\frac{1}{2}$–1 in) across, come above the surface in spring. All these species can be propagated from cuttings. H.

R. flabellaris (*R. delphinifolius*) is N. American, its bright green branching stems thickly clothed with leaves repeatedly divided into hair-like, submerged segments 2.5–7.5 cm (1–3 in) long. The floating leaves, roughly an inch across, are cleft into linear segments. Small yellow flowers star the water.

ROTALA *(Lythraceae)*

Several members of this genus are now stocked by aquatic dealers for cultivation in tropical aquaria. They need temperatures around 22°C (72°F) or a little over.

R. rotundifolia from S.E. Asia is the best known and has ovate submerged leaves of a reddish colour in whorls of three. Emergent leaves are produced if the light is good and the water not too deep. These are rounded and opposite, with small violet flowers in the axils. *R. macranda* from India is similar. *R. indica* from Asia and southern Russia has purplish-violet flowers and oval, egg-shaped, opposite and reddish-green submerged leaves. T.

SAGITTARIA *(Alismataceae)* arrowhead *(see p. 69)*

Sagittarias are of interest because of the various leaf shapes adopted by many species. They are usually related to the age of the plant or the depth of water covering the tubers. Juvenile leaves are normally narrow and ribbon-like—well adapted to an aquatic existence, particularly in running water. These have some value for oxygenating purposes. However, after a time the plant develops broader and more rounded leaves which float on, or are borne just above the surface, and finally produce free-standing aerial foliage which is markedly arrow-shaped with long basal lobes and pointed tips. The plants are perennial from walnut-sized tubers produced at the ends of subterranean runners, which can be detached for propagation purposes. These tubers contain starch and are edible; in the United States those of *S. latifolia* are eaten as a vegetable by local Indians and immigrant Chinese and called duck potatoes.

S. engelmanniana, from the U.S.A. where it flourishes as a bog plant, may be used in cold aquaria or placed outside in summer to grow as a marsh plant. It then produces arrow-shaped leaves and white, three-petalled flowers in whorls on 45 cm (18 in) stems. C.

S. graminea, also N. American, from Florida to Newfoundland, grows 10 cm (4 in) to 60 cm (2 ft) in height according to how it is grown. In shallow water whorls of white flowers and long-stemmed, narrowly oval leaves are produced. In deeper water the rosettes of membranous, ribbon-like leaves make good oxygenators. C.

S. lancifolia (*S. falcata*), a handsome N. American marsh plant, will grow 120–150 cm (4–5 ft) in an outdoor pool, but in a cold water tank produces abundant grassy juvenile leaves, particularly in the subspecies var. *angustifolia* and var. *media*. C.

S. latifolia (wapato or duck potato) is very variable and has a number of synonyms like *S. gracilis*, *S. hastata* and *S. simplex*. It can be used in aquaria but makes a better showing as a pondside aquatic. N. America. C.

S. platyphylla has egg or heart-shaped (never arrow-shaped) leaves. The species comes from the southern U.S.A. and is useful in warm or cold aquaria for its broad, submerged juvenile foliage. T.

S. sagittifolia (see p. 70), a common plant of northern Europe, is specially cultivated for its edible tubers in China and Japan. In aquaria it is important to keep plants at the juvenile stage, usually achieved by growing them in poor light, poor soil and deep water. C.

S. subulata (*S. natans*). N. and S. America. Popular on account of its diminutive juvenile foliage which rarely exceeds a few inches in height. Its simple grassy leaves can carpet a small aquarium, excellent cover for tiny fish. T & C.

SAMOLUS *(Primulaceae)* water pimpernel
S. parviflorus (*S. floribundus*) (underwater rose), N. America. A small moisture-loving perennial growing to 60 cm (2 ft) with about 8 cm (3 in), spoon-shaped, simple leaves and terminal racemes of small white flowers. Sometimes used in aquaria, or planted in boggy places. H.

TYPHONIUM *(Araceae)*
These are Asian plants, fairly new to cultivation but now coming in fairly regularly to the aquarium trade. The species have small tubers, long petioled, arrow-shaped leaves and purplish arum flowers. They will grow submerged or emerged. *T. flegelliforme* from Malaya has 20–25 cm (8–10 in) leaves on longer petioles. Propagated by division. T.

UTRICULARIA *(Lentibulariaceae)* bladderwort
There are 120 species of bladderworts, the majority tropical bog plants growing in soil, often with spikes of handsome flowers resembling antirrhinums. Only a few are genuinely aquatic, some European, including British. These aquatic forms have no roots and need no special cultivation beyond still, clean water. Small water creatures such as water-fleas (daphnia and cyclops) are trapped in bladders occurring on their leaves and stems. Each of these has a movable flap and spiny hair-like appendages on the outside. The bladders are only partially filled with water, the quantity controlled by small organs attached to their sides,

and when a water creature touches one of the spiny appendages the bladder flap rapidly gives way, allowing water—and the victim—to rush inside. This wave of water rebounding against the inner wall of the bladder causes the flap to close again, trapping the animal, which then dies.

It is not known which, if any, part of the victim is absorbed by the plant nor why it captures certain kinds of creatures only to leave others—of the same size —untouched.

According to Dr. de Wit in *Aquarium Plants*, some species of S. American utricularias are found only in the vase-shaped receptacles formed by the leaf bases of certain bromeliads.

U. vulgaris, the largest and best known European species, floats just under the water surface, its large forked leaves divided into many hair-like segments carrying the bladders. In summer the blooms appear, six or eight together on spikes above the water; bright yellow with two orange lips and a spur on each. Later in the year the plant develops 'winter buds', which are really detached shoot tips carrying a number of dormant, closely packed leaves. These sink into the mud at the bottom of the pool and restart into growth the next spring. C.

U. minor, also European, is similar but very much smaller.

There are also a number of N. American aquatic bladderworts which rarely, if ever, find their way into dealers' premises so are not readily obtainable. C.

VALLISNERIA *(Hydrocharitaceae)* eel grass, ribbon grass, tape grass
Probably the best-known and most important aquarium plants, easy to grow, readily procurable and good oxygenators. They have submerged, ribbon-like leaves of varying widths and small but interesting blooms.

V. spiralis is the commonest in cultivation. Male and female flowers are borne on separate plants, the former at the base of the leaves resembling small, white, stalked bags. These contain many simple flowers—in bud—and when conditions are right the membranous bag bursts and the bud quickly rises to the surface. Here they open, the three to four small petals curl backwards and they form a platform on which two pollen-topped stamens rest. The female flowers are quite different, each being carried at the end of a long spiral stalk which wends its way to the surface when ready for pollination. At the tip of this is a green bract containing three stigmas. If any of these are touched by a floating pollen-bearing male flower, fertilization is achieved; after which the spiral stem contracts and the seeds ripen under water. In parts of N. America another species, *V. americana*, is freely planted in nature reserves where it makes valuable food for the canvas-back duck and other waterfowl which eat both the seeds and succulent shoots. It is sometimes called 'wild celery', because it is claimed it imparts a celery-like flavour to the flesh of birds which feed upon it. All vallisnerias increase vegetatively by means of runners which can be severed and replanted. Vallisneria grows fairly well in sand at the bottom of aquaria, but will do better if there is a layer of loam beneath the sand.

V. americana, from the Atlantic U.S.A., Mexico and Jamaica, has rosettes of rough, pale green, ribbon-like leaves up to 90 cm (3 ft) long. T.

V. gigantea, New Guinea, Philippines, Australia and Tasmania. A broad-leaved species with dark green, strap-shaped leaves which can reach 180 cm (6 ft) in length and are 3–5 cm ($1\frac{1}{4}$–2 in) wide. Needs a large aquarium, temperatures 18°C (64°F) and over. T.

V. spiralis, southern Europe and N. America. Bright green leaves, sometimes twisted, up to 80 cm (2 ft 8 in) long, 4–8 mm ($\frac{1}{6}$–$\frac{1}{3}$ in) wide. A form occurs, *V.s.* var. *tortifolia* (or *torta*), with slightly broader leaves, twisted for the whole of their length, like a corkscrew. It is shorter growing than the species. Another species, *V. asiatica* (*V. natans*), from Asia, is very similar to, and often confused with, *V. spiralis*. T.

ZANNICHELLIA *(Zannichelliaceae)* horned pondweed
Z. palustris, a slender, sparsely branched plant, of creeping habit and fragile to handle. Leaves opposite, linear, flat; flowers inconspicuous. Usually found in brackish water. Cosmopolitan. C.

9

Floating aquatics

Floating aquatics are particularly important to aquarists for not only do they make an attractive finish to a well-planted aquarium, but they provide shade from excessive toplight and sanctuary for certain small forms of animal life which in due course become food for fishes. Some floaters are important aerators, holding bubbles of oxygen for a long time—even far into the night, until they are gradually absorbed by the water. Some tropical fish will build their nests among floating plants while the trailing roots of others, like pistia and eichhornia, make nurseries for egg layers.

In the garden, floating aquatics spread rapidly in warm weather and can become a nuisance if allowed to get out of control. For this reason all members of the duckweed family (*Lemna* sp.) should be banned. It is true that they keep the water clear beneath them through the shade they cast, and also provide food and shelter for countless small creatures, but once introduced, they are almost impossible to eradicate later. Always a few stray fronds remain to reinfect the pond as soon as conditions allow.

Floating aquatics present no planting or propagation problems; simply float them on the water. They grow quickly and are readily separated if further plants are required.

AZOLLA *(Azollaceae)* fairy moss
A. caroliniana and *A. filiculoides*, both S. American and almost identical in appearance, form mats of small lacy fronds which are only 5–7 mm ($\frac{3}{8}$ in) long and pale green in summer, but red, crimson and brown towards autumn. Both spread rapidly but are killed by frost. A few stock plants can be over-wintered in a pan of loam covered with an inch of water; also a few plants usually survive in outdoor pools in mild winters.

CERATOPTERIS *(Parkeriaceae)* floating fern
Aquatic, rather succulent tropical ferns, submerged or floating, with long, dangling, finely divided roots. There are two species, closely related and difficult

to distinguish. To do well they need a temperature around 20–22 °C (68°–72 °F).

C. thalictroides (water sprite), S.E. Asia. Deeply divided sterile fronds 45 cm (1½ ft) long and 25 cm (10 in) wide of pale green, standing 50–70 cm (20–28 in) above the water. Fertile fronds narrower with baby plantlets along the edges which can be separated for propagation purposes.

C. cornuta, Africa. Considered by some authorities to be a form of preceding, has simple leaves barely divided.

C. pteridoides, S. America. Broad floating fronds with a few incisions.

EICHHORNIA *(Pontederiaceae) (see also p. 61)*

E. crassipes (water hyacinth), S. America. Introduced to many tropical countries where it sometimes flourishes to such an extent that river navigation is impeded. Not frost hardy, in cool climates it must be overwintered in a large warm water aquarium or else be potted in soil and kept just damp in a greenhouse until spring. The smooth cordate leaves grow in rosettes, each leaf stalk swollen like a sausage and filled with spongy tissue full of air which enables it to float. These grow 5–15 cm (2–6 in) tall and in the centre of the rosettes 15 cm (6 in) spikes of 10–30 large and showy flowers appear in summer. Individually, these are light purplish blue with six perianth lobes, the uppermost of which bear conspicuous gold and blue peacock eye markings. Long purplish roots trail down, sometimes a metre (3¼ ft), and these are much favoured by goldfish varieties as repositories for their eggs. The plant increases by means of stolons, like strawberry plants.

HYDROCHARIS *(Hydrocharitaceae)* frogbit

H. morsus-ranae, Europe. A practically rootless aquatic with small, round, fleshy floating leaves each about 2.5 cm (1 in) across, in rosettes, and three-lobed white flowers in spring, male and female on different plants. It does not spread greatly but in summer multiplies by means of horizontal stolons which have new plants at their ends. In autumn large buds form on these stolons, then fall off and lie all winter in the mud, sprouting in spring.

HYDROCLEYS *(Hydrocleis) (Butomaceae)*

H. nymphoides (Limnocharis humboldtii) (water poppy). A small genus of S. American perennials with long trailing stems, occasionally rooting, with milky sap and thick, oval to heartshaped leaves 5 cm (2 in) across and clusters of large, showy, three-petalled yellow flowers, 5–6 cm (2–2½ in) across, standing clear of the water. These last for only a day but are constantly renewed all summer. The plant needs warm temperate conditions or can be grown in tubs with a loam base or in indoor pools or large aquaria. It needs plenty of light and makes a good companion for tropical water lilies. Both leaves and stalks contain spongy tissue which enables them to float. Propagated by division or cuttings.

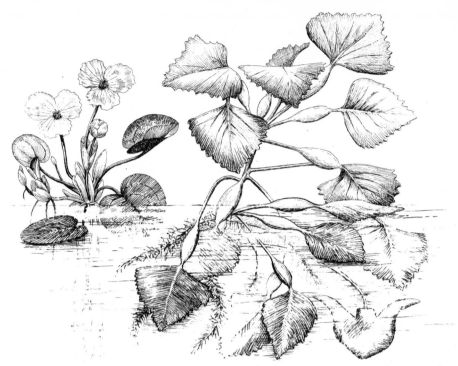

Left: *Hydrocharis morsus-ranae*, right: *Trapa bicornis*

LIMNOBIUM *(Hydrocharitaceae)* American frogbit
L. spongia, tropical America. A perennial floater, stoloniferous, with long-petioled, kidney-shaped leaves up to 10 cm (4 in) long, green, spotted with reddish-brown above, but having spongy tissue below which makes them buoyant. Flowers unisexual, insignificant. Useful in aquaria but needs good lighting and a temperature of 20–22°C (68–72°F).

    L. laevigatum (commonly known as *L. stoloniferum*) *(Trianea bogotensis),* Mexico, Brazil. Similar to preceding but leaves smaller, to 2.5 cm (1 in) and more compact. Propagated by division.

LURONIUM See p. 93

NEPTUNIA *(Leguminosae)* water sensitive
N. oleracea, tropical America. Long floating stems which root at the nodes and are covered with spongy tissue full of air cells to keep them afloat. Leaves deeply cut, very like those of *Mimosa sensitiva,* and similarly sensitive when touched. Flowers in heads 2 cm ($\frac{3}{4}$ in) long, bright yellow at the top, brown beneath. Propagated by seeds.

PHYLLANTHUS *(Euphorbiaceae)*
P. fluitans, S. America. A unique plant belonging to the same family as the

poinsettia; the species a free floating aquatic very like salvinia (below), with crimson, conspicuously veined leaves about 15 mm ($\frac{3}{5}$ in) in diameter, which age to a velvety green. As the young leaves lie partly overlapping the older ones this results in a most attractive colour combination. Flowers small and whitish; and red, fibrous trailing roots. Not frost hardy.

PISTIA *(Araceae)* water lettuce
P. stratiotes, tropics and subtropics. A stoloniferous floater forming rosettes up to 15 cm (6 in) across of pale green, fan-shaped, velvety leaves. Roots trailing and feathery, up to 15 cm (6 in) long. Flowers small and inconspicuous. In the Far East the species is often cultivated to encourage the breeding of edible water shrimps; and also mixed with rice to feed ducks and pigs. In some places it is a serious pest, but being frost sensitive must be overwintered in warmth in cool climates. A useful aquarium plant for fish breeders.

RICCIA *(Ricciaceae)*
R. fluitans (crystalwort), widespread in tropical waters. A very small, much branched, floating liverwort, 15 mm ($\frac{3}{5}$ in) long and 1 mm ($\frac{1}{24}$ in) wide, pale green, occurring in groups. Popular for tropical aquaria; not frost hardy.

RICCIOCARPUS *(Ricciaceae)*
R. natans (Riccia natans) A small aquatic liverwort, the only species in the genus and widespread in the tropics. Although it has a land form the plants are usually found floating, the thallus rounded or triangular, about 5–10 mm ($\frac{1}{5}$–$\frac{2}{5}$ in) wide and bright green. It is sometimes grown in tropical aquaria.

SALVINIA *(Salviniaceae)* water velvet
These S. American fern allies form groups of unwettable, ear-shaped, velvety leaves, about 1 cm ($\frac{3}{8}$ in) long, covered with fine silky hairs. These are two-ranked, pale green and soft to the touch. There are also submerged, finely dissected leaves lying under the floating leaves which resemble roots. The plants need plenty of light and water rich in nutrients. The plants are not hardy so stock pans should be kept in a greenhouse over winter.

    S. natans of southern Europe, *S. auriculata* and *S. oblongifolia*, both S. American, are the kinds most frequently offered by aquatic dealers.

STRATIOTES *(Hydrocharitaceae)* water soldier, water aloe
S. aloides, Europe. This looks like the leafy top of a pineapple with spiny rosettes of green, narrow, serrated leaves 5–20 cm (2–8 in) long and 10–20 cm (4–8 in) wide; the three-parted 2.5 cm (1 in) flowers are white, male and female being borne on separate plants. It floats just under the water, coming up to bloom in late summer, then sinking to the bottom of the pool. A good oxygenator for outdoor pools, propagated from side shoots.

TRAPA *(Onagraceae)* water chestnut
T. natans. An annual from southern Europe with long, creeping, submerged stems 60 cm (2 ft) or so long, bearing triangular, chocolate-mottled green, dentate leaves upheld as floaters by means of spongy leafstalks. The small white insignificant flowers come in late summer and are succeeded by large black edible seeds which have four stout spines or projections—hence another common name, water calthrop. The seeds are also used for rosaries.

 T. bicornis has two-horned fruits and is eaten as a vegetable or preserved in honey in China and Korea, while *T. maximowiczii*, also from Asia, has four thin, slightly curved horns, about 5 × 2.5 cm (2 × 1 in). Propagated from seed.

TRAPELLA *(Pedaliaceae)*
T. sinensis. A Chinese annual with elongated, slender stems, the submerged leaves lanceolate, the floating leaves rounded and toothed, upheld by swollen footstalks as in trapa. The pale rose flowers are tubular with five divisions and succeeded by curious fruits with two long, slender spines. Needs warm conditions; propagated by seeds.

10

The bog garden

A bog garden is a marshy or wet area of ground which rarely dries out and hardly ever becomes waterlogged, except for brief periods. Its soil remains constantly moist, an essential condition for certain plants and conducive to better growing conditions with others. Included among the latter are several herbaceous perennials which are normally grown in borders, like astilbes, trollius and *Iris sibirica*. If the roots of these are dry they fail to give of their best, but in bog gardens they are invariably tall and fine.

However, bog plants are not aquatics. They need to feel the influence of water without sitting in it for long periods, the main factors for success being plenty of moisture plus a situation usually (but not always) fully exposed to the sun. It follows that the bog garden should be constructed in a low-lying area, not at the top of a slope, nor in a shady corner.

Some gardens possess an open site where water collects naturally. Given this, very little extra preparation is necessary beyond providing manure and adding water in times of drought. The same principle applies to gardens through which a stream flows. However, the vast majority of gardens possess neither of these advantages so a bog has to be created.

Constructing the bog

There are several ways of making a bog, using either concrete or clay or an artificial liner. As with pool construction, the latter is the most efficient, also simplest and cheapest. In every instance first excavate the soil to a depth of 45 cm (18 in). On heavy soil you will probably come down to pure clay at that level, so if you want to make a clay lining some can be removed and worked with water—like plasticine—to form a mastic-like substance. This is then used to line the sloping sides. Use more water to keep the clay damp and beat it down frequently and firmly with a heavy rammer. The idea is to make a watertight basin. Incidentally, it will be found that it is easier to work with clay in dry weather.

Pontederia cordata. Blue flowers are uncommon in the water garden so this north American native is a 'must'. It flowers in late summer and has glossy heart-shaped leaves.

Hydrocleys nymphoides. The water poppy flowers right through the summer, carrying its three-petalled, golden-yellow flowers just above the surface.

If you prefer concrete the excavation must be deeper (60 cm or 2 ft) and the cavity lined with 15 cm (6 in) of a mixture made up (by bulk) from one part cement, two parts sharp sand and three parts washed shingle. Smooth this over the bottom and sides and after 24 hours fill the basin with water, for concrete sets better under water, and only remove this when you are ready to add soil and plants.

For a plastic liner apply the same technique as advocated for pool liners (p. 10), tucking the spare edges of material out of sight beneath rocks or soil. Incidentally, with any of these methods the bog can be made to any shape or size required. If the site naturally attracts water make holes 15 cm (6 in) down from the top of the plastic liner or concrete. This will allow flood water, heavy rains and the like to seep away from the plant roots.

Filling

Most bog plants need a humus-rich soil but first fill the bottom of the basin with 10 cm (4 in) of stones, broken brick or hardcore for drainage. Cover this with 10–12 cm (4–5 in) of chopped turves, leaves or any moisture retentive organic material. Pack this well down before adding good loam or garden soil mixed with sharp sand or grit, leafmould or peat and some *well-rotted* garden compost or farmyard manure.

In later seasons an annual spring mulch of compost, leafmould or peat will keep the soil fertile.

Raise the level of the bog garden so that the soil stands well above that of the surrounding garden. This will enable the plants to obtain moisture by capillary action without being over-wet at the roots. A few stepping-stones will make it easier to attend to plants in wet spots. When the bog is combined with a rockery feature a few pieces of rock should be introduced to create continuity.

Water can be supplied via a small pipe attached to a mains tap hidden by rocks or plants. In large gardens it may be necessary to have several inlets but with very small gardens it may be enough just to top them up from time to time with a hose. Whichever way water is added, however, aim at a gentle trickle rather than a fast jet.

The plants

Many of the poolside aquatics described in Chapter 8 will thrive also in bog gardens, particularly species of kingcups, bogbeans, bog arums, *Iris pseudacorus* and flowering rushes. Insectivorous plants will grow in such situations as well as certain bulbs, shrubs, ferns, reeds and the like (see Chapter 11). I have grouped these plants in categories which should make them easier to find in plant catalogues. Small trees and shrubs can be planted beyond the bog and watered with a hose or the bog can be flooded over from time to time if this seems necessary. Tree roots go down more deeply if they are not confined and will not damage the bog liners. Apart from their natural beauty a few trees or shrubs make useful windbreaks to shelter the water garden.

Perennials for bog gardens

ACONITUM *(Ranunculaceae)* monkshood, wolf's bane
A genus of hardy border perennials for rich, moist soil which are easily naturalized beside streams and pools. The hooded flowers contain long-stalked nectaries to attract insects for pollination purposes and the deeply cut leaves are smooth and shiny but the tuberous roots are poisonous, containing poisonous alkaloids. An infusion of *A. napellus* was once used to poison criminals. For this reason they should never be planted where they might be dug up by mistake for culinary purposes, such as mistakenly for horse radish. Aconitums may require staking and since they come through the ground early in the year are best transplanted in autumn. They bloom in summer and are propagated by division and seeds.

   A. × cammarum. All plants of garden origin, mostly hybrids of *A. napellus ×* *A. variegatum* with glossy, palmate leaves. Notable varieties are 'Newry Blue', dark blue, 90–150 cm (3–5 ft); 'Bressingham Spire', very erect, violet-blue; 'Ivorine', creamy-white; 'Bicolor', deep blue and white; and 'Spark's Variety' (*A. henryi*), very dark navy blue, 120–150 cm (4–5 ft).

   A. carmichaelii (A. fischeri). A splendid plant from Kamtchatka, long grown in gardens (it was introduced in 1886), with rich blue, hooded flowers on 45 cm ($1\frac{1}{2}$ ft) stems. 'Kelmscott' is similar but richer in colour.

   A. napellus from N. Europe is an erect plant, 90–120 cm (3–4 ft) tall with narrowly divided leaves and light indigo-blue flowers. The British representative of this species is given independent rank by some botanists as *A. anglicum*. It has been cultivated in gardens since the 16th century and at one time the dried roots were used as a heart and nerve sedative and as a pain reliever.

   A. paniculatum from S. Europe grows 90–120 cm (3–4 ft) tall with spreading branches and soft violet flowers. It normally requires staking.

   A. variegatum, eastern Alps, has parti-coloured flowers of blue and yellowish blue, or sometimes plain violet; also wiry stems and pinnately lobed leaves.

   A. volubile from E. Asia and Siberia is a distinct plant of climbing habit, the slender, twining stems clambering up other plants to a height of 120 cm (4 ft) in late summer. The purplish or blue and green flowers are small, about 4 cm ($1\frac{1}{2}$ in).

ACTAEA *(Ranunculaceae)* baneberry
Useful plants for front row positions in cool, moist, partially shaded situations. The small white flowers, borne in terminal racemes in spring, are succeeded by bright berries. Leaves large, compound, something like those of buttercups (*Ranunculus* sp.). Although the berries are poisonous, a tincture made from

them is used to relieve various medical conditions including angina, dropsy, whooping cough and muscular rheumatism. The plants are propagated by division in spring or by seed sown directly after harvesting.

A. *pachypoda* (*A. alba*) (white baneberry), N. America. White flowers on 30–60 cm (1–2 ft) stems; white, pea-sized berries on red footstalks.

A. *rubra* (red baneberry, snakeberry), N. America. Similar to preceding but with scarlet berries; 45 cm (1½ ft).

A. *spicata* (herb-Christopher), Europe, S.W. Asia. Purplish-black berries; flowers white or bluish; 60 cm (2 ft).

ALETRIS *(Liliaceae)* star-grass, unicorn root

A. *farinosa*. Forms thin, grassy tufts from the centres of which rise 60–90 cm (2–3 ft) spikes of 12 mm (½ in), white tubular flowers in late spring and early summer. Useful for colonizing in moist, sunny positions. The plant comes from eastern N. America where the brittle roots are dried and used medicinally. Propagated by seed or division.

ANEMONE *(Ranunculaceae)* windflower

Anemones are very variable, both as regards habit and soil requirements. While most of them need sharp drainage and frequently partial shade, there are several better suited to the deep, damp soil of the bog garden. These can be propagated by seeds or division, preferably in early spring.

A. *narcissiflora*, Europe and Asia, has three to five parted, basal leaves and branching heads of 2.5 cm (1 in), white, buttercup-like flowers in early summer. Height 45–60 cm (1½–2 ft).

A. *rivularis*, India, Ceylon. A handsome plant for naturalizing at the waterside, growing about 60 cm (2 ft) high with branched stems of white flowers, which have blue exteriors and blue anthers.

A. *virginiana* (thimbleweed), N. America, grows 30–45 cm (1–1½ ft) high with several white or greenish-white flowers about 4 cm (1½ in) across and deeply cut leaves. Occasional flooding will not damage the plants.

ARUNCUS *(Rosaceae)* goat's-beard

A. *dioicus* (*A. sylvester, Spiraea aruncus*), temperate regions of Europe and Asia, Alaska. A noble plant for the waterside, grown either in groups or as a solitary specimen. The heavy trusses of creamy-white flowers grow to 1.8 m (6 ft) in summer and have a rich, hay-like scent. The male plants are usually the most feathery, but the females have attractive seedheads which can be used for dried arrangements. The large leaves are deeply cut pinnately and have long stems up to 120 cm (4 ft) around the flower spikes. The form known as A. *d. astilboides* is identical but smaller, growing 60 cm by 45 cm across (2 ft by 1½ ft), and 'Kneiffii' has deeply cut and dissected foliage. All can be propagated by division and are suitable for partial shade in moist soils.

ASCLEPIAS *(Asclepiadaceae)* milkweed, silkweed

Summer blooming plants, mostly from N. America and Africa, usually with milky sap and simple leaves, alternate or in whorls on the stems. Several are suitable for the vicinity of the water garden.

A. incarnata (swamp milkweed), N. America. A stout-stemmed perennial 90–150 cm (3–5 ft) tall, well-clothed with opposite, oval-elliptic leaves and inflorescences of pink flowers. These each have five projecting horns (sources of honey), reflexed petals and a five-parted stigma. The stems contain a fibre, the roots are used for various ailments like asthma and rheumatism and the buds are reputedly eaten by N. American Indians.

ASTER *(Compositae)* starwort, aster

Mostly plants for well-drained borders or rock gardens with a few native to boggy areas in N. America and Europe. These are useful for their late blooms, which come at a time when most bog plants are fading. The plants are propagated by division.

A. nemoralis (N. American bog aster) grows 15–60 cm (6–24 in) with slender leafy stems carrying 4 cm ($1\frac{1}{2}$ in) heads of pink or violet-purple flowers.

A. puniceus (red-stalked aster or swan weed), from N. American swamps, grows quite tall in nature, 2.4 m (8 ft), but about 75 cm ($2\frac{1}{2}$ ft) in cultivation. It has reddish stems, oblong, smooth leaves and violet, lilac, pink or white, daisy-like flowers.

A. tripolium (sea aster), Europe, Asia, N. Africa. A short-lived perennial to 90 cm (3 ft), carrying smooth, linear, fleshy leaves and corymbs of small purplish flowers with yellow centres.

ASTILBE *(Saxifragaceae)*

Ideal herbaceous perennials, long-lasting with branching heads of spiraea-like flowers borne on tapering panicles in shades of pink, crimson and white. These never require staking. Handsome, compound leaves which make splendid ground cover and a foil for the feathery inflorescences. The old brown seedheads can be cut for dried arrangements or left to ornament the winter landscape. Astilbes are of easy cultivation, thriving in most soils provided they have plenty of water. They can also be lifted and forced under glass, taking 14–16 weeks to flower by this technique. There are very many hybrids and varieties, many of French and German origin. These should be propagated by division, the species by seeds or division.

A. × arendsii. A collective name, honouring Georg Arends of Ronsdorf, who carried out much hybridizing work with astilbes, particularly *A. japonica*, *A. chinensis* var. *davidii*, *A. thunbergii* and *A. astilboides*. The hybrids come in various heights, 60–120 cm (2–4 ft) and 30–45 cm (1–$1\frac{1}{2}$ ft), and different colours. Among the most readily obtainable, which have stood the test of time and bloom in summer, are:

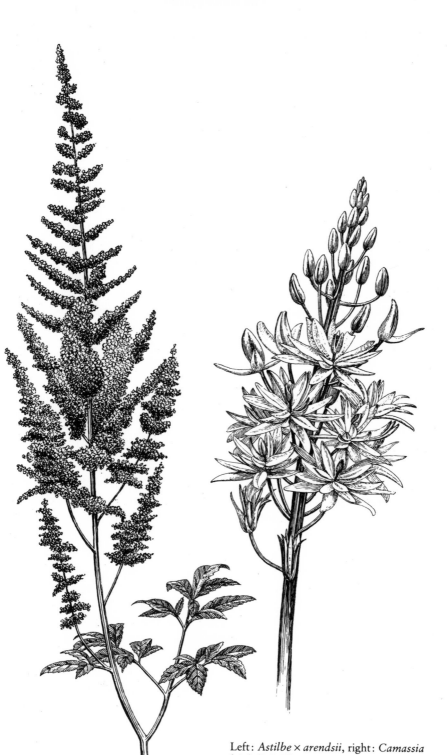

Left: *Astilbe* × *arendsii*, right: *Camassia leichtlinii* 'Plena'.

Medium-tall 'Bridal Veil' 75 cm (2½ ft), 'White Gloria' 60 cm (2 ft), early, and 'Silver Sheaf' 90 cm (3 ft), all white; 'Betsy Cuperus' 75 cm (2½ ft), pale pink; 'Erica' 90 cm (3 ft), bright pink; 'Lilli Goos' 90 cm (3 ft), rose-pink, very late; and 'Gunther' 90 cm (3 ft), bright pink; 'Bremen' 75 cm (2½ ft), salmon-crimson; 'Fanal' 60 cm (2 ft), crimson-red, early; 'Granat' 105 cm (3½ ft), deep crimson; 'Koblenz' 60 cm (2 ft), salmon; and 'Salland' 1.8 m (6 ft), magenta.

Short 'Bronze Elegance' 30 cm (1 ft), clear pink; 'Praecox Alba' 30 cm (1 ft), white; 'Serenade' 45 cm (1½ ft), clear pink, very late; 'Sprite' 45 cm (1½ ft), soft pink.

 A. chinensis var. *davidii* originated in China and has rosy-purple flowers.

 A. grandis, China. A tall species, up to 1.8 m (6 ft) with large, deeply cut leaves and yellowish-white flowers on long, branching panicles.

 A. japonica (*Spiraea japonica*). A well known Japanese species, the florists' spiraea; often used for forcing, growing to 90 cm (3 ft) with white flowers.

 A. rivularis, Himalayas. A fine foliage plant, to 1.5 m (5 ft), with compound leaves and 8 cm (3 in), ovate leaflets and large sprays of creamy-white flowers.

 A. simplicifolia, Japan. A dwarf species with simple, ovate, deeply lobed leaves and short panicles of white, starry flowers. Height 22.5 cm (9 in). There is a rose-pink form.

 A. thunbergii, a graceful Japanese species for the waterside, growing about 75 cm (2½ ft) with white flowers which often become rosy with age. It is of bold, erect habit and does well in light shade.

ASTRANTIA *(Umbelliferae)* masterwort
Interesting European plants with quaint inflorescences consisting of heads of minute flowers set off by collars of chaffy bracts. They thus resemble miniature Victorian posies. The plants need plenty of moisture, being among the first plants to show signs of drought. They are suitable for full sun or partial shade and are of erect growth with handsome, lobed, buttercup-like leaves and aromatic roots. The plants make dense clumps which spread by means of underground runners. Propagated by division or seed.

 A. carniolica, from the European Alps, grows about 30 cm (1 ft) tall and has blush-rose flowers with green and white striped bracts.

 A. major is a taller plant, to 60 cm (2 ft). An Austrian species, with curious green and pink flowers and five-lobed leaves. A form called 'Rubra' has crimson flowers and another, 'Sunningdale Variegated', has cream-splashed variegated foliage.

 A. maxima (*A. helleborifolia, A. heterophylla*), also European, is a charming species with pink flowers which have rose collars. It is a good plant to set by water in light shade. Grows about 60 cm (2 ft) tall.

 A. minor from European mountain areas is a dwarf species only 15–22 cm (6–9 in) high, with umbels of white flowers.

BOLTONIA *(Compositae)*

Boltonias resemble michaelmas daisies and in damp situations are of the easiest cultivation in sun or shade. They make large plants of branching habit, which need staking as they sprawl about but are ideal for wild garden areas where they can be left to colonize. Propagation is by division.

B. *asteroides*, from N. America, grows to 1.8 m (6 ft) with alternate, sessile, lanceolate leaves and white, lilac or purplish flowers, which are larger and deeper coloured in var. *latisquama*.

B. *decurrens*, N. America, has branched heads of white, lilac or purple daisy flowers 1.5–1.8 m (5–6 ft) tall.

BOYKINIA *(Saxifragaceae)*

B. *aconitifolia* comes from the eastern U.S.A. and likes moist, cool, lime-free soil, in partial shade. It grows about 60 cm (2 ft) tall, with a creeping rhizome, toothed or lobed, rounded basal leaves and branching heads of small, yellow-centred, white, five-petalled flowers in summer. Propagated by division or seeds.

BRUNNERA *(Boraginaceae)*

B. *macrophylla* (*Anchusa myosotidiflora*). This well-known plant with its rough heart-shaped leaves and sprays of bright blue forget-me-not flowers is ideal for damp spots in the bog garden. Suitable for light to full shade, it blooms in spring but is apt to spread rapidly unless regularly culled. There is a cream variegated-leaved form called 'Variegata', which is less rampant but prone to sun and wind damage so has to be carefully sited. Propagated by division.

BULBINELLA *(Liliaceae)*

B. *hookeri* (*Chrysobactron hookeri*). A New Zealand plant suitable for bog gardens in sun or partial shade. It flowers in early summer, the smooth 60–90 cm (2–3 ft) stems carrying spires of starry yellow flowers, above grassy tufts of narrow strap-shaped leaves. A peculiarity of the species is the extreme brittleness of the fleshy roots, which are as fragile as glass so need careful planting. Propagated by seeds or division.

BUPHTHALMUM *(Compositae)* oxeye

B. *salicifolium*. A coarse but striking European plant, growing 60 cm (2 ft) tall and flowering in late summer. The yellow daisy heads, over 5 cm (2 in) across, persist for weeks. Leaves oblong-lanceolate. Propagated by division or seeds. Seedlings bloom in their first season.

CAMASSIA *(Liliaceae)*

North American bulbous plants, ideal for naturalizing in moist situations and good for cutting. In their native habitat the bulbs are often under water at flowering time in early summer. They should be planted 7–10 cm (3–4 in) deep and left undisturbed. The bulbs of some species are cooked and eaten by N. American Indians. Propagated by division or seeds.

C. *leichtlinii* is the best and most robust species, growing 90 cm (3 ft) tall with lax grassy leaves and terminal racemes of creamy-white flowers in early summer. Forms exist with pale to deep blue flowers like the deep blue 'Suksdorfii' and the double primrose-yellow 'Plena', which comes true from seed. In our garden the latter spreads freely in borders, shrubberies and even rose beds.

C. *quamash* is the edible quamash or camosh, a robust species about 60 cm (2 ft) high with white, pale blue or blue-violet flowers.

CARDAMINE *(Cruciferae)* cuckoo flower, lady's smock
Dainty spring-flowering perennials, Tennyson's 'faint sweet cuckoo flowers' are particularly suitable for the lower reaches of the bog garden. They are of easy cultivation and propagated by division.

C. *pratensis*. The common lady's smock of English meadows with pinnate, cress-like smooth leaves, which were once used in salads, and rosy-lilac flowers on dainty 15–23 cm (6–9 in) sprays. The double form 'Plena' is the better plant. Occasionally the leaves root and make young plants.

C. *trifolia* from Switzerland is similar, with white flowers.

CARDIOCRINUM *(Liliaceae)*
Suitable only for large gardens with deep, damp, humus-rich soil, these giant lilies are sensational when in bloom, and even after flowering with their large brown seed pods. I once saw several hundred, some 3.6 m (12 ft) tall, growing together in a wet woodland in New Zealand and I shall never forget the sight. Normally they grow up to 3 m (10 ft) with large heart-shaped leaves about 30 cm (1 ft) long and thick spikes of 20 or so white, fragrant, downward-pointing, trumpet flowers 15 cm (6 in) long. The bulbs die after flowering but increase naturally from offsets. Plant these shallowly in light dappled shade.

C. *giganteum* (*Lilium giganteum*) from W. China is the most imposing.

CHAMAELIRIUM *(Liliaceae)* blazing star, wand lily
C. *luteum*. A N. American tuberous-rooted plant growing 30–90 cm (1–3 ft) tall with tufts of plantain-like leaves and in early summer slender spikes of yellowish-white flowers. The dried roots have medicinal properties. It needs a moist shady situation and is propagated by seed or division.

CHELONE *(Scrophulariaceae)* turtlehead, snakehead
Handsome, late-summer, N. American perennials native to swamps and damp woods. They are propagated by seed or division.

C. *glabra* grows about 60 cm (2 ft) in Britain but reputedly up to 1.8 m (6 ft) in the wild. It has lanceolate or ovate leaves and white or pink, hooded flowers which resemble the head of a turtle, in spire-like racemes.

C. lyonii forms masses of nearly cordate leaves and has terminal heads of reddish-purple flowers on 60 cm (2 ft) stems.

C. obliqua is purple-flowered and 60 cm (2 ft) tall with lanceolate elliptic leaves.

CHRYSANTHEMUM *(Compositae)*

Two chrysanthemum species, both European, grow well in very moist soil so can be planted for their late summer blooms, which make useful cut flowers.

C. lacustre, the marsh oxeye daisy from Portugal, is a robust perennial, 120–150 cm (4–5 ft) tall with rough, sharply toothed leaves and 8 cm (3 in) white flowers with yellow centres.

C. serotinum (*C. uliginosum*) from Yugoslavia also has white flowers on branching sprays 1.2–2.1 m (4–7 ft); these always turn to face the sun.

CHRYSOSPLENIUM *(Saxifragaceae)*

C. americanum (golden saxifrage, water carpet). A N. American native of little value except for carpeting wet, muddy places near ponds. It is a succulent, semi-aquatic plant with small, green, rounded, toothed leaves and very small greenish flowers in early spring.

C. oppositifolium is its European counterpart. In the Vosges the leaves are used for salads under the name of Cresson de Roche. Both species can be propagated by division.

CIMICIFUGA *(Ranunculaceae)* bugbane

Although not strictly bog plants, cimicifugas make attractive background plants for cool, moist places at the back of a wild garden. In spite of their height they do not need staking and they flower in late summer or autumn. Propagated by division.

C. americana (summer cohosh), N. America. A tall species, to 1.8 m (6 ft), with basal leaves having three leaflets and the pinnate, upper ones three to five leaflets, also long racemes of small, white flowers—like bottlebrushes.

C. dahurica from Manchuria, grows 90–150 cm (3–5 ft), with wide branches of fluffy white flowers.

C. foetida from Asia and Siberia has feathery plumes of creamy-white to yellow flowers on 90–180 cm (3–6 ft) stems. It has an unpleasant foetid odour. The roots are used medicinally in China.

C. racemosa (black cohosh, black snakeroot) is so called because it is said to cure snakebites. The roots are also used to improve the appetite and for various medicinal purposes. It comes from N. America and grows 90–240 cm (3–8 ft) tall with dense wand-like spikes of white bottlebrush flowers on branching stems and dark green leaves. *C. cordifolia* has deeply cordate, terminal leaflets.

C. simplex, Asia. A smaller species, rarely more than 120 cm (4 ft), with arching wands of flowers. It has several cultivars, notably 'White Pearl', 'Elstead Variety' and 'Braunlaub', a German form with brownish leaves.

CLAYTONIA *(Portulacaceae)*
C. virginica (spring beauty). A delightful N. American with linear basal leaves and racemes of pink-tinged, white flowers. It is a succulent plant, the leaves of which are sometimes eaten like spinach. It has corms and can be propagated from offsets of these or seeds.

CLINTONIA *(Liliaceae)*
Charming small perennials for moist shady places with rhizomatous roots, mostly basal leaves and terminal umbels of small, six-petalled flowers. Both mentioned are N. American.

C. borealis (corn lily, bluebead). Has glossy oblong leaves, greenish-yellow flowers and blue berries. 45 cm (1½ ft).

C. umbellulata (speckled wood lily). Oblong leaves, green and purple spotted white flowers followed by black fruits. 45 cm (1½ ft).

COPTIS *(Ranunculaceae)* goldthread
These small perennials are all natives of the northern hemisphere and, like most members of the buttercup family, thrive in damp soil. They also favour light shade and are evergreen with shiny, usually trifoliate leaves and slender rhizomes which yield a yellow dye and have medicinal uses. They are propagated by seeds or division of the clumps.

C. trifolia from N. America and N. Asia grows 10–15 cm (4–6 in) high and has slender stems carrying solitary, white, 5–7 petalled flowers with yellow basal spots.

COREOPSIS *(Compositae)*
C. rosea (pink tickseed). A N. American perennial growing to 60 cm (2 ft) with opposite, entire, two or three parted leaves and branching stems carrying yellow-centred, pink daisy flowers each about 25 mm (1 in) across. It is suitable for an open, moist position, is stoloniferous and propagated by division.

DENTARIA *(Cruciferae)*
D. heptaphylla (*D. pinnata, Cardamine heptaphylla*) (toothwort). A handsome, spring-flowering perennial from the damp mountain valleys of the European Alps, which will grow in deep shade and flowers very early in spring. Invaluable for undercarpeting shrubs as well as in the environs of the water garden. Growing about 50 cm (20 in) tall, it has light green, deeply cleft, palmate leaves and terminal racemes of large, pure white flowers. These are similar to but larger than those of cardamine (p. 116). The plants have curious, tooth-shaped, white, fleshy rhizomes—hence the common name. Propagated by division.

Other species are the European *D. enneaphyllos* with creamy flowers, *D.*

pentaphyllos (*D. digitata*) lilac-flowered (also European) and *D. californica* from N. America, white to purple.

DIPHYLLEIA *(Berberidaceae)*
D. cymosa (umbrella leaf). A N. American perennial growing to 90 cm (3 ft) with large basal leaves which each have two lobes and can be up to 60 cm (2 ft) across. The small white flowers occur in rounded heads and are succeeded by 12 mm ($\frac{1}{2}$ in), indigo-blue berries on red stalks. It needs cool damp soil and light to strong shade. Propagated by division or seeds.

DODECATHEON *(Primulaceae)* shooting star
These well known, mostly N. American, spring-flowering plants, which have their floral parts reflexed like those of a cyclamen, are found wild in very wet meadows. They dislike dryness at the roots but leafy or peaty soil conditions with reasonable drainage and some shade suit them well. Some have plain green, strap-like leaves, others mottled foliage, and most grow around 30–37 cm (12–15 in) high. Propagated by seeds or division.

    D. frigidum has mauve-violet flowers and plain leaves; *D. hendersonii* is purple and yellow; *D. meadia* has purple spotted leaves and magenta flowers, also forms like 'Alba', white, and 'Brilliant', rosy-crimson.

EOMECON *(Papaveraceae)*
E. chionanthum. A Chinese plant commonly known as poppy-of-the-dawn with branched stems containing orange-red sap, round, smooth, long-stemmed basal leaves and white, poppy-like flowers on 45 cm ($1\frac{1}{2}$ ft) stems in spring. It needs cool moist soil in shade and is propagated by division.

EPILOBIUM *(Onagraceae)*
E. angustifolium (*Chamaenerion angustifolium*) (rose-bay willow herb, fire-weed). A showy plant, widely spread in the northern hemisphere but too weedy to be introduced indiscriminately as underground runners cause the plant to spread rapidly and it also seeds freely. The silky appendages of the seeds have been used for lamp-wicks in Lapland and also spun—with poor success—into cloth. The leaves are also used in Asia to make tea. Goats, cows and sheep are said to eat the plant as fodder and the silky down surrounding the seeds mixed with fur is made into stockings and other clothing by Lapps. The plant grows 120–150 cm (4–5 ft) tall with narrow, dark green leaves and showy spikes of rosy, sweet-smelling flowers. There is a sterile, white-flowered variety called 'Album', beautiful to look at and very slow to spread since it sets no seed. This one must be propagated by division.

ERICA *(Ericaceae)* heather
A number of heathers can be introduced with charming effect to the bog garden,

where on rocky banks or sloping mounds they form their own adornment. Among the most suitable for such positions are forms of the rosy-flowered *E. carnea*, winter flowering and the cross leaved or bog heather *E. tetralix*, with soft pink flowers all summer. Both are European and are propagated by layers or cuttings.

ERYNGIUM *(Umbelliferae)* sea holly
There are many eryngiums but the best for damp soils are *E. aquaticum* and *E. yuccifolium*, very similar N. American species which are often sold under the last name. Growing 90–120 cm (3–4 ft) tall, with long, linear, prickly-edged leaves, the flowers are whitish on branching stems and consist of rounded, thistle-like inflorescences. The roots are used by Indians to treat kidney complaints, or candied for sweetmeats. They need moist soil and flower in late summer. Propagated by division.

EUPATORIUM *(Compositae)*
Coarse perennials having rigid stems with leaves mostly opposite or arranged in whorls, either simple or dissected, also large terminal heads of purple, white or rose flowers. They appreciate plenty of moisture, flower in summer or early autumn and are propagated by division.

E. *cannabinum* from Europe, N. Africa and W. Asia is called hemp agrimony and can become invasive. It grows 120 cm (4 ft) high with purplish flowers, which are double in 'Plenum'.

E. *purpureum*, the Joe Pye weed, is N. American and has 180–240 cm (6–8 ft) stems of purplish-rose flowers on dark purplish stems in autumn. There is a white form. The bruised leaves smell of vanilla.

EUPHORBIA *(Euphorbiaceae)* spurge
E. *palustris*. Although this European species will grow in ordinary well-drained borders it makes a much finer specimen when planted in boggy ground in sun or light shade. It is an imposing plant, 90 cm (3 ft) tall, with leafy stems and rich yellow flower bracts in spring which remain weeks in character. Propagated by division.

FILIPENDULA *(Rosaceae)* meadow sweet
Plants once known as spiraeas, a name now more properly assigned to shrub species. Most of them delight in moist, rich soil in sun or semi-shade and flower in summer. Meadow sweets are especially decorative when grown near water, in positions where the feathery plumes of flowers may be advantageously reflected. The nomenclature of filipendulas is confused and many have been grown in gardens under incorrect names. As far as possible I have given alternatives but these names may again be altered in the future by botanists. They are propagated by seed sown in spring or by division.

F. *kamtschatica* (*Spiraea palmata*). A native of Kamtchatka and Manchuria, this fine species may be described as a giant meadow sweet, growing 1.8–3 m (6–10 ft) tall with dark green, pinnate leaves and panicles of white, fragrant flowers.

F. palmata from Siberia and Kamtchatka grows to 90 cm (3 ft) with pale pink flowers which fade to white.

F. rubra (*Spiraea lobata, Ulmaria rubra*) (queen of the prairie), N. America. A magnificent plant up to 1.5 m (5 ft) tall, with large, pinnately divided leaves and fragrant, rosy-carmine flowers in summer. 'Venusta' is especially fine with deep rose flowers.

F. ulmaria (*Spiraea ulmaria*) (queen of the meadow), Europe (including Britain), Asia. A well known ditch species native to Britain with divided basal leaves and plumes of creamy, fluffy flowers on 90–150 cm (3–5 ft) stems. Even more attractive are *F.u.* 'Variegata' which has creamy-yellow leaf variegations, 'Plena' with double flowers and 'Aurea' with golden leaves.

GENTIANA *(Gentianaceae)*

Several gentians will grow in the better drained areas of the bog garden, where they provide interesting features in late summer or early autumn. They should be given deep rich, lime-free soil, and are propagated by seed or spring cuttings.

G. asclepiadea (willow gentian). A European species with willow-like leaves,

Gentiana asclepiadea

arching 60 cm (2 ft) stems bearing axillary pairs of rich blue trumpet flowers in autumn. There is a white form. Willow gentians associate pleasantly with ferns in light shade.

 G. *lutea* (great yellow gentian) is found wild in European meadows and damp places in woods and on mountain sides. It grows from 45–180 cm (1½–6 ft), with stout stems, large rounded leaves and dense axillary and terminal whorls of golden yellow flowers. It relishes good deep soil and sun, and flowers in mid-summer. The plant is the source of gentian root used medicinally and in the preparation of vermouth.

GEUM *(Rosaceae)*
G. *rivale* (water avens) is a plant of the northern hemisphere, including Britain, where it is found in damp or marshy places. It has strawberry-like leaves and dull purplish-pink flowers on 45–60 cm (1½–2 ft) stems. Forms occur with pinkish-orange flowers like 'Leonard's Variety', or yellow in 'Lionel Cox'; these are better for garden use. Propagation by division.

GUNNERA *(Haloragaceae*, sometimes referred to *Gunneraceae)*
Handsome foliage plants, 1.5–3 m (5–10 ft) high, that create an inimitable air of grandeur at the waterside. The simple leaves are the largest among land plants, resembling gigantic rhubarb, 180–240 cm (6–8 ft) across, deeply lobed and bristly on prickly leaf stems. In early summer the greenish-brown flowers come in long, 90–120 cm (3–4 ft) spikes—like huge pipe-cleaners. In a large garden a single plant of the Brazilian G. *manicata* looks extremely impressive sited by running water or in a damp bog. When frost blackens the leaves the crowns must be protected from further cold by heaping them over with these leaves. Pile straw and dry leaves over these and leave until spring when the covering can be removed. Propagated by division.

 G. *chilensis* (G. *scabra*, G. *tinctoria*) from Patagonia grows 90–180 cm (3–6 ft) but is otherwise very similar, and there is a low-growing, stoloniferous species, G. *magellanica*, from the Falkland Islands and Patagonia, which makes fine ground cover in colder climates.

HACQUETIA *(Umbelliferae)*
H. *epipactis* (*Dondia epipactis*). An interesting rather than spectacular little plant from the European Alps, for cool, moist, peaty soil. The slender stems carry rosettes of greenish-yellow flowers, something like astrantia blooms, and have radical, trifoliate leaves 7–15 cm long. Propagated by division in spring.

HELONIAS *(Liliaceae)* swamp pink
H. *bullata*. An uncommon N. American bog perennial growing 30–60 cm (1–2 ft) tall (90 cm/3 ft in nature) with oblong, spoon-shaped leaves and spikes of fragrant pink or purplish flowers. Propagated by division.

HELONIOPSIS *(Liliaceae)*
Plants for cool, moist but well drained soil so keep plants in the drier part of the bog.

H. orientalis from Japan and Korea grows to 30 cm (1 ft) with radical, oblanceolate leaves up to 10 cm (4 in) long and up to 10, rose-purple flowers on spikes; *H.o. breviscapa* has creamy-white or rose flowers.

HEMEROCALLIS *(Liliaceae)* day lily
Invaluable for bog and water garden settings, with a long flowering period since as each bloom dies another takes its place. The flowers appear in summer and are trumpet-shaped, in various shades of yellow and orange, also pink, apricot, salmon and maroon-red in garden hybrids. The leaves are arched and broadly grassy; the height of the branching flower stems is from 60–150 cm (2–5 ft) according to variety. In nature they are found on stream-sides, particularly in China and Japan where the dried flowers are packaged and sold as gum tsoy (golden vegetable) or gum jum (golden needles) for use in salads. When these are soaked in water they become gelatinous and are then used for soups and meat dishes.

The following species and forms are commonly cultivated, although gardeners should visit a nursery when the varieties are in flower and plant a selection of these. Most are summer flowering. Propagation by division.

H. aurantiaca, China, orange, 90 cm (3 ft); also 'Aurantiaca Major', with larger flowers; *H. citrina*, China, 90 cm (3 ft), citron-yellow; *H. dumortieri*, Japan, Korea, 60 cm (2 ft), yellow, early spring; *H. flava* (*H. lilio-asphodelus*), Europe and Asia, 75 cm ($2\frac{1}{2}$ ft), clear yellow, sweetly scented; *H. fulva*, Japan, orange-brown, 120 cm (4 ft), and its forms 'Rosea', soft glowing rose, and 'Kwanso Flore Pleno', a double orange splashed with red and copper; *H. middendorffii*, Asia, orange-yellow, fragrant, 30–60 cm (1–2 ft); *H. minor*, Siberia, a dwarf, 30–45 cm (1–$1\frac{1}{2}$ ft), clear yellow, scented, late spring; and *H. thunbergii*, Japan, Korea, 60–90 cm (2–3 ft), fragrant, lemon-yellow flowers.

HERACLEUM *(Umbelliferae)* cow parsnip, cartwheel plant
H. mantegazzianum (giant hogweed), Caucasus. An immense plant which is monocarpic so dies after flowering. It has large compound leaves, 90 cm (3 ft) across, on red-flecked stems and compound umbels of white flowers up to 120 cm (4 ft) across in summer. Suitable for deep, moist soil in sun or shade where bold effects are required.

This species and *H. stevenii* seed freely after flowering so should have the heads removed after blooming to prevent this. Some people's skin is allergic to the sap.

H. stevenii (*H. laciniatum*, *H. giganteum*, *H. villosum*), Caucasus. A species masquerading under various names and a bold subject for the waterside, growing 240–360 cm (8–12 ft) high with enormous plate-like flower heads and

Left: *Hemerocallis fulva*, right: *Hosta fortunei* 'Marginato-alba'

huge, lobed leaves. Toy popguns are sometimes fashioned from the hollow stems. Propagated from seed.

The boiled leaves and seeds of another European species, *H. sphondylium*, are used in the making of liqueurs in France and central Europe.

HIBISCUS *(Malvaceae)*
A large family of mostly warm temperate and tropical species, a few of which are native to swamps. The latter seem to do better in the United States than in northern Europe, and are often planted in containers stood in pools so that the base is just covered with water. They are highly ornamental for warm temperate climates with large, showy, rounded, mallow flowers in summer. They are worth trying in temperate gardens. Propagated by seed for species, cultivars by means of cuttings.

H. moscheutos (swamp rose mallow), eastern U.S.A. A strong perennial up to 180 cm (6 ft) or more with lanceolate to ovate, simple or 3–5 lobed leaves to 20 cm (8 in) long and solitary, satiny white, pink or rose flowers up to 15 cm (6 in) across with crimson bases. There are many named cultivars in various shades.

HOSTA (FUNKIA) *(Liliaceae)* plantain lily
An invaluable group of plants for woodland or waterside planting, with bold, prominently veined, basal leaves which are attractive even when out of bloom. The flowers are drooping and often fragrant, of tubular shape with six segments in terminal racemes in mid to late summer. Most are native to Japan, a few to China and Korea. Plantain lilies should be planted in deep, rich but not water-logged soil in dappled shade and left alone to grow to big clumps. The genus is much confused as regards names, especially in gardens. Propagate by removing sections of old clumps in spring; try to do this without disturbing the main plant.

H. crispula (Funkia sieboldiana var. *marginata).* A striking plant growing up to 90 cm (3 ft) when well established with wavy-margined, ovate leaves and trumpet-shaped, lavender flowers.

H. decorata, 60 cm (2 ft), lilac-flowered, leaves ovate to elliptic, dark green with broad white margins carried right down the leaf-stalks.

H. elata (H. fortunei var. *gigantea),* a robust 90 cm (3 ft) or more plant, with plain green, wavy-edged, long-pointed, ovate leaves to 25 cm (10 in) long; flowers lilac-lavender.

H. fortunei (Funkia fortunei). A very old garden plant, clump-forming and about 60 cm (2 ft) high. Leaves ovate, to 13 cm (5 in), plain sage green; flowers pale lilac to violet. Cultivars include 'Aurea', with young yellow leaves which become green with age; 'Albopicta', soft yellow leaves edged with pale green which deepen with age until the leaves have two distinct tones of soft and darker green—an outstanding form; and 'Marginato-alba', whose sage-green leaves are white-edged.

H. lancifolia (*Funkia* and *Hosta japonica*), a narrow-leaved species, has ovate lanceolate, glossy, dark green, 13 cm (5 in) blades; flowers deep violet.

H. longissima (*H. japonica* var. *longifolia*), 17–18 cm (7 in), spoon-shaped to linear lanceolate leaves of plain green; flowers pale rosy-purple, very late. Height 45 cm (1½ ft).

H. plantaginea (*Funkia subcordata*), known as the fragrant plantain lily because of the lily-like scent emanating from the 12.5 cm (5 in) white flowers, especially towards evening. Leaves oval-rounded, yellow-green and glossy; late blooming; 60 cm (2 ft). There is reputed to be a double-flowered form but I have never seen it; also a form known as *H.p. grandiflora* with narrower leaves and flowers.

H. rectifolia, 90 cm (3 ft), flowers cobalt-blue; leaves plain green.

H. sieboldiana (*H. glauca*), 75 cm (2½ ft). This has the largest leaves, up to 37.5 cm (15 in) long, glaucous green, heavily ribbed; flowers whitish-lilac. There are cultivars with yellow leaf margins.

H. sieboldii (a confusing name with similarity to preceding and sometimes called *H. marginata* or *Funkia ovata albomarginata*), 75 cm (2½ ft). Has puckered, elliptic-ovate leaves, green with white margins; flowers violet, up to 30 on one stem.

H. undulata (*Funkia undulata*), 60–90 cm (2–3 ft). 15 cm (6 in), elliptic to ovate leaves striped lengthwise with yellowish-white; dark green, very twisted edges. Flowers lilac.

H. ventricosa (*H. caerulea*, *Funkia ovata*). To 120 cm (4 ft) with heart-shaped, wavy-edged, deep green, shiny leaves; bell-shaped, violet flowers with darker veining. Forms with yellow leaf marbling, 'Aureo-maculata', and cream edging, 'Variegata', occur.

IMPATIENS *(Balsaminaceae)* balsam, busy Lizzie

Some impatiens are perennial, others annual, but most like damp to wet conditions. In Europe they are usually raised from seed, self set, or sown either outside or in pots (planted out later) according to where one lives. One of the most reliable for banks of streams and bog gardens is *I. glandulifera* (*I. roylei*), a Himalayan 180 cm (6 ft) or more annual with ovate-lanceolate leaves on succulent stems and axillary racemes of three or more, large, white, pink, red or near purple flowers. The plant has become naturalized alongside many European and American streams and rivers.

I. wallerana (*I. holstii*, *I. sultanii*) is the busy Lizzie or patient Lucy, widely grown as a house plant. The plant comes from Tanzania and varies in height from 10–13 cm (4–5 in) in some of the newer varieties to 60–90 cm (2–3 ft). The flowers may be white, pink, carmine-purple, orange or combinations of these.

Modern varieties of the plant grow in sun or shade provided the soil is damp, and flower all summer. Not frost hardy.

INULA (*Compositae*)

Showy perennials with yellow 'daisy' flowers. The following are suitable for the bog garden and can be propagated by division.

I. helenium, Europe. Often called elecampane, this species grows 90–150 cm (3–5 ft) high with very large, wrinkled, oblong leaves, downy beneath and 75 mm (3 in), bright golden flowers in late summer. The roots have medicinal properties and are used for chest and lung complaints.

I. hookeri, China, has small, oval, hairy leaves on branching 75 cm ($2\frac{1}{2}$ ft) stems and light yellow flowers. It is inclined to spread so keep in check.

IRIS (*Iridaceae*)

A genus containing many species and varieties suitable for waterside planting. Most appreciate some humus in the ground but dislike lime. Propagated by seed (a slow method) or division of the roots.

From the swamps of S.E. U.S.A. have come a number of beautiful species, notably *I. fulva* and *I. giganticaerulea*, some of which have hybridized to make natural hybrids or colour forms. There are too many of them to mention so only the most important and readily available kinds are included here. Most flower early to mid summer.

I. bulleyana, China, 45 cm ($1\frac{1}{2}$ ft), grassy leaves, rich blue flowers, with cream, purple-veined falls.

I. chrysographes, China, 45 cm ($1\frac{1}{2}$ ft), narrow leaves, flowers deep velvety purple with gold veining.

I. delavayi, a native of the Yunnan marshes in China, 90–120 cm (3–4 ft), hollow-stemmed, flowers 50–65 mm ($2-2\frac{1}{2}$ in) across, violet with white markings.

I. forrestii, China, 60 cm (2 ft), lemon-yellow with brown veining, narrow leaves, hollow stems.

I. fulva (*I. cuprea*), copper iris, 60 cm (2 ft), flowers copper-red, two or three blooms on each stem. A U.S.A. swamp species with thin, narrow leaves.

I. giganticaerulea. A tall species from U.S.A. swamps, grown more there than in Europe; narrow leaves, 150 cm (5 ft) stems, musk-scented, violet-blue flowers with yellow blotches on falls.

I. kaempferi. The clematis-flowered irises of Japan are by far the most striking group for bog gardens, the colours varying from white, cream and yellow to different shades of blue, violet, crimson and red-purple. Since the falls rarely droop but instead are held horizontally the large, often bicoloured blooms resemble giant patterned butterflies when seen from a distance. They prefer a sunny position by the waterside, with plenty of water during the growing season, but drier conditions in winter. This can be achieved by flooding over the growing area in summer. They like a rich soil, but lime is fatal. The species is frequently confused with *I. laevigata*, a true aquatic (p. 62), but can be distinguished if the fingers are run the length of the leaves. Those of *I. kaempferi*

Left: *Iris sibirica*, right: *Iris kaempferi*

have a prominent midrib which is lacking in *I. laevigata*. There are countless varieties, some double; often with Japanese names.

I. lacustris (lake iris). A small iris, under 30 cm (1 ft), found by gravelly lakeside shores in N. America. Flowers sky-blue, about 50 mm (2 in) wide, in spring with a repeat flowering in autumn.

I. sibirica, central Europe. A slender, graceful species, free-flowering and adaptable, the blooms long-lasting when cut and mostly in shades of blue. The roots form a dense spreading mat, the arching green leaves grow in tufts and the flowers stand erect on wiry 90–120 cm (3–4 ft) stems. They will grow in a dry border but give a much better display in wet ground. Some of the sturdiest and best coloured are 'Snow Queen', white; 'Perry's Blue', pale blue; 'Helen Astor', plum-red; 'Sea Shadows', deep blue; and 'Marcus Perry', near navy.

I. versicolor, N. America, is best represented by its variety 'Kermesina', a 60 cm (2 ft) plant with vivid claret-magenta flowers, reticulated with white.

I. virginica comes from southern U.S.A. marshes and has sword-shaped, arching leaves and two or three lavender-lilac and yellow-blotched flowers on 60–90 cm (2–3 ft) stems.

KIRENGESHOMA *(Saxifragaceae)* yellow waxbells
K. palmata, Japan. An outstandingly beautiful plant for early autumn flowering, a time when many others have passed from bloom. In our garden it flowers in deepest shade but is equally happy in dappled light, provided the soil is always moist. Growing 60–120 cm (2–4 ft) high, it is of spreading habit with dark purple stems, large thin, jagged leaves something like maple leaves and loose sprays of pendent, 5 cm (2 in), shuttlecock-shaped flowers of brightest yellow. Propagated by division or seed.

LIGULARIA *(Compositae)*
Summer flowering, daisy type plants of robust habit, sometimes coarse but always showy. Ideal for moist ground in sunny places; if dry at the roots they soon collapse. Propagated by seed or division.

L. dentata (Senecio clivorum). A Chinese species with large, shiny green leaves, almost round and up to 30 cm (12 in) across on long stalks. The stout green, 90–120 cm (3–4 ft) stems support branching heads of rich orange flowers from mid to late summer. 'Orange Queen' has larger blooms; 'Desdemona' has purple stems and lower leaf surfaces; 'Othello' is similar but less purple; and 'Gregynog Gold' is a hybrid 180 cm (6 ft) tall with huge leaves and spikes of orange flowers.

L. japonica from Japan grows 120–150 cm (4–5 ft) with round-oval leaves, cut into three segments, and heads of orange-yellow, 10 cm (4 in) flowers.

L. macrophylla (Senecio ledebourii) from the Altai Mountains of Asia is a large plant with leaves like horse-radish, up to 60 cm (2 ft) long, and dense inflorescences of canary-yellow flowers.

L. przewalskii (*Senecio przewalskii*) from N. China is one of the loveliest. It has deep purple, rather slender stems carrying many thin, palmately-lobed leaves and 120–180 cm (4–6 ft), thin spires of small yellow flowers. It soon collapses in drought.

L. vetichiana and *L. wilsoniana* (giant groundsel) are both Chinese and each grows around 180 cm (6 ft) tall. They have large, almost round leaves and branching stems with golden daisy flowers.

LOBELIA *(Campanulaceae)*

The perennial species of this genus make striking waterside plants, especially when grouped where their reflections can be seen in water. They are all summer flowering, liking rich soil and sun, and can be propagated by seed, division or cuttings.

L. cardinalis (cardinal flower). A N. American species growing 90 cm (3 ft) tall, forming rosettes of green, oblong leaves with toothed margins and vivid scarlet, salvia-like flowers on green stems.

L. fulgens from Mexico is not quite as hardy as preceding but very similar except that it has crimson stems and often reddish leaves. In America this species is referred to *L. splendens*. It is the parent of many fine cultivars like 'Queen Victoria' and 'Bees' Flame', both scarlet flowered with deep crimson leaves; 'Will Scarlett', bright red; 'Huntsman', scarlet. In cold districts the plants are sometimes killed in winter—easily avoided by lifting a few roots in autumn or striking some cuttings, and keeping them in a frame until the next year.

L. syphilitica (blue cardinal flower). N. American species growing 60–90 cm (2–3 ft) tall with 5–10 cm (2–4 in), lanceolate leaves and dense racemes of blue flowers, much smaller than those of preceding species. There is a form with white flowers. The species crossed with *L. cardinalis* cultivars has produced some striking colours. These are commonly listed as *L. × gerardii* or *L. × vedrariensis*. They grow 45–60 cm ($1\frac{1}{2}$–2 ft) tall with purple or crimson-violet flowers, one named 'Tania' being crimson-purple. It was raised at E. A. Bowles's garden at Myddelton House, Enfield, quite near our home.

LYSICHITON *(Araceae)*

L. americanum. A handsome, N. American aroid with deep butter-yellow flowers in early spring appearing before the leaves. These are about 30 cm (1 ft) high with a rather unpleasant scent; the oblanceolate leaves are up to 120 cm (4 ft) long and 30 cm (1 ft) wide.

L. camtschatcense from Japan is similar but white-flowered and rather smaller with a pleasant scent. Both species propagate from self-set seedlings and will grow in swamps or wet ground.

LYSIMACHIA *(Primulaceae)* loosestrife

Useful and easily grown plants for damp soil; all mentioned here being propagated by division and flowering in summer.

L. ciliata (Steironema ciliata), N. America, naturalized in Europe. A 90–120 cm (3–4 ft) perennial with opposite, ovate-lanceolate leaves, 10 cm (4 in) long, and many, slightly nodding, 25 mm (1 in), light yellow flowers.

L. clethroides, China, Japan. Grows to 90 cm (3 ft), with ovate-lanceolate leaves tapering at both ends and long pendent spikes of small white flowers.

L. punctata, Europe, naturalized in N. America. Inclined to be invasive, the species grows to 120 cm (4 ft) with whorled or opposite lanceolate leaves and axillary whorls of bright yellow flowers.

L. thyrsiflora, a swamp species from Europe, Asia and N. America. Of creeping habit from rhizomes; 60 cm (2 ft) tall leafy stems and short, axillary spikes of pale yellow blooms.

L. vulgaris (great yellow loosestrife). A common European, including British, plant with leafy panicles of bright yellow flowers and tapering leaves; 90 cm (3 ft).

LYTHRUM *(Lythraceae)* purple loosestrife
Natives of low-lying wetlands and ideal for massing in wild garden settings. All are easily reproduced by division and flower in late summer.

L. salicaria. A showy plant of the Old World, naturalized in N. America and growing 120 cm (4 ft) or more in height, the woody stems bearing linear to oblong leaves. The slender downy spikes support many reddish-purple terminal and axillary flowers, which are eclipsed in beauty by such cultivars as 'Robert', clear pink; 'Firecandle' ('Feuerkerze'), rich rosy-purple; 'Lady Sackville', rosy-red; and 'Morden's Pink', pink.

L. virgatum, Asia Minor, is similar but smoother than preceding, with more pink in the flowers. 'Dropmore Purple' is purplish and 'Morden Gleam', deep rose pink. 90–120 cm (3–4 ft).

MECONOPSIS *(Papaveraceae)*
These beautiful plants are mainly Asiatic and make perfect associates for hardy ferns and bog primulas. They require soil which is moist but not wet, especially during the growing season; rather drier in winter. Plenty of humus—peat or leafmould—with a generous helping of coarse sand should be dug into the ground beforehand, when they should be planted so that the crowns are just level with the soil surface. They abhor lime and like cool conditions—the roots go down deeply, so should be given some shade in areas exposed to bright sunshine or drying winds. Leave undisturbed when happily established. Propagated from seed sown immediately after harvesting or in the case of cultivars by careful division.

M. betonicifolia (M. baileyi) (Himalayan blue poppy). A superb plant, 120 cm (4 ft) or more in height with oblong, toothed leaves all the way up the stems and in early summer several large, 5 cm (2 in), cup-shaped, four-petalled flowers filled with a mass of golden stamens. In the best forms the flowers are a brilliant electric blue, although sometimes purplish or a washy mauve. The species is usually (but not always) monocarpic and dies after flowering. Graham Thomas (*Perennial Garden Plants*) says the best colour forms probably come from the topmost seedpod.

M. *cambrica* (Welsh poppy). A British native and an inveterate seeder once it becomes established. Growing 30–45 cm (1–1½ ft) tall, it has pinnately divided, ferny leaves and saucer-shaped, stamen-filled flowers of vivid lemon or bright orange in late spring. There are double forms of both. These have to be increased by division.

M. *chelidoniifolia*, China. A distinct species of branching habit with smaller but many more flowers than M. *grandis* and M. *betonicifolia*. They are nodding, bell-like and pale yellow, with pinnately-lobed, stalked, basal leaves and sessile stem leaves; 90 cm (3 ft); early summer.

M. *grandis*, Himalayas, has very large, four-lobed, deep blue flowers on 90–150 cm (3–5 ft) stems and rosettes of hairy, oblanceolate, toothed leaves. It is a variable plant however and purplish blooms can appear. Some of these have been named and there is a white called 'Puritan'. The species has hybridized with M. *betonicifolia* to produce a race called M. × *sheldonii*. Mr Thomas thinks the exquisite blue cultivar known as 'Branklyn' rightly belongs here. This has blooms up to 20 cm (8 in) across in early summer.

MIMULUS *(Scrophulariaceae)* musk
Showy moisture-loving annuals and perennials which provide a riot of colour throughout most of the summer. Western N. America is especially rich in species although Britain has but one representative, the common naturalized monkey musk, M. *guttatus*. This species, crossed with various Chilean types, like the copper-red M. *cupreus*, has produced some splendid dwarf cultivars in a wide range of colours which can be planted near water and are easily raised from seed or cuttings. They will not survive hard winters so must be renewed most years.

M. × *burnetii*. A hybrid musk with the habit of M. *luteus*. Of tufted habit it has copper-yellow flowers, spotted with brown and yellow throats. Propagated by division.

M. *cardinalis*, N. America, 90 cm (3 ft). An erect and sticky perennial with hairy, 10 cm (4 in), oblong leaves and in summer scarlet to pale reddish-yellow flowers like antirrhinums.

M. *lewisii*, western N. America. Sticky, very hairy, greyish, oblong leaves and 5 cm (2 in), deep rose to pink, occasionally white, flowers in summer; 60 cm (2 ft).

M. *luteus*, Chile. Yellow flowers blotched with red and smooth, ovate, toothed leaves; 30 cm (1 ft). This species will grow in shallow water; summer.

M. *ringens*, eastern N. America, will also grow in shallow water and has an erect, square stem, 30–60 cm (1–2 ft) high, carrying oblong, mostly sessile, serrate leaves and axillary, 35–40 mm ($1\frac{1}{2}$ in), blue or bluish-violet, two-lipped flowers in summer.

MONARDA *(Labiatae)* bee-balm, bergamot, Oswego tea
M. didyma. Robust, square-stemmed plants with brilliant flowers, found growing by N. American streams and lakes. Massed in the bog garden they create striking effects, with their vivid scarlet, salvia-like flowers, especially when they are sited against a dark background. The 90 cm (3 ft) stems bear nettle-like leaves which are fragrant when bruised and were once used in America for tea. Moist soil is essential. Many cultivars were raised in Kent, England, just prior to World War II, some of the best still widely grown. Examples are 'Cambridge Scarlet', brilliant red; 'Croftway Pink', rose-pink; 'Prairie Night', purplish; 'Snow Maiden', white; and 'Violet Queen', violet. Some of these may be derived from the very similar *M. fistulosa*, another N. American. All flower in summer and can be propagated by cuttings or division.

PELTIPHYLLUM *(Saxifragaceae)* umbrella plant
P. peltatum (Saxifraga peltata), California. The common name is descriptive since the great 30 cm (1 ft) in diameter leaves of this species, poised like teatrays on 90 cm (3 ft) stems, do indeed resemble umbrellas. The pink flowers appear first, in early spring, in rounded heads atop rosy-tinted stalks. The plants need deep wet soil, in sun or shade, and can be propagated by division.

PHORMIUM *(Liliaceae)* New Zealand flax
Phormiums are not really bog plants, although in New Zealand they are commonly found in places which lie wet for much of the year. Large specimens are planted in prominent poolside situations in the milder counties of the British Isles, also in Ireland, mainly for the striking effect of their magnificent sword-shaped leaves. Unless protected (e.g. with bracken) they are not hardy in very cold winters. Some growers keep them in containers, sinking these in wet ground for the summer, then lifting and taking them under cover for winter.

  P. tenax is a valuable fibre plant and has also been employed medicinally, a decoction of roasted, macerated roots being applied to abscesses and unbroken chilblains. Maoris are said to have once made love tokens from slips of the leaves. A double slip-knot was so made that when tightly pulled it ran into one large single knot. The Maori brave gave this to the lady of his choice, who signified her consent by pulling the two knots into one.

  P. tenax grows up to 3 m (10 ft) tall, its smooth leaves impossible to tear across horizontally, although they shred lengthwise with ease. The skirts of Maori maidens were fashioned from these strips. The purplish flower stems grow several feet taller and bear numerous dull red and yellow tubular flowers. 'Purpureum' is a cultivar with reddish-purple leaves; 'Variegatum' is longitudinally striped in cream and green; and of recent years others have been

Left: *Lobelia cardinalis*, right: *Monarda didyma*

introduced from New Zealand, with orange-tinged leaves or in mixtures of red, green, salmon and bronze, also dwarf types. The latter may owe their reduced height to the similar but shorter at 120 cm (4 ft) *P. cookianum*. All flower in late summer and are propagated by division.

PHYSOSTEGIA *(Labiatae)* obedient plant
P. virginiana, E. U.S.A. Called obedient because individual blooms can be moved around the flower spikes and stay where put. The plants grow 30–120 cm (1–4 ft) tall, the tallest in very damp soil and sun. They have running rootstocks so rapidly make bold colonies if left undisturbed. The toothed, smooth, nettle-like leaves are 75–125 mm (3–5 in) long and the sage-like, bright rosy-pink flowers appear mid to late summer. 'Vivid' is a particularly fine form and there is one with white flowers. Propagated by division.

PHYTOLACCA *(Phytolaccaceae)* poke weed, red ink plant
Coarse perennials for damp rather than boggy soil, but capable of growing in rough and shady situations. They reach 120 cm (4 ft) tall and have oblong lanceolate leaves and 15 cm (6 in) spikes of white or purplish flowers in early summer, which go on to produce rather striking displays of dark purple berries, filled with red juice. Although the plants are poisonous the young shoots are cooked and, after the water which absorbs the toxic properties has been discarded, they are eaten as greens in N. America. The plant is also unpleasantly smelly. It can be propagated by seed or division.

    P. americana (*P. decandra*) from America and *P. clavigera* from China are the most frequently grown.

PODOPHYLLUM *(Berberidaceae)* may apple
Interesting rather than spectacular perennials, but useful for damp, shady places. They have fleshy roots from which is derived the drug podophyllin, used medicinally since very ancient times. In spring, quite suddenly the folded leaves come through the ground and rapidly grow to 45 cm (1½ ft). They are umbrella-shaped and deeply lobed, about 25 cm (10 in) across. Just beneath them and on the same stem occur six-petalled, white, pink or red flowers which later develop to edible, plum-like fruits. Propagation by seed or division.

    P. hexandrum (*P. emodi*) from the Himalayas has rich bronze and red spotted leaves in pairs and 5 cm (2 in) white or pinkish flowers, with red fruits.

    P. peltatum, N. America, has one solitary 5 to 9 lobed leaf, a white flower and a rosy-yellow fruit.

POLYGONUM *(Polygonaceae)* knotweed
Strong-growing annuals and perennials of easy cultivation, most requiring moist soil. Often decorative but inveterately persistent when once established so apt to become invasive. They are propagated by seed or division.

P. affine comes from the Himalayas where it grows on river banks and even hangs in rosy clumps from moist precipices. It grows to 45 cm (1½ ft) with radical, 10 cm (4 in), evergreen, tapering leaves and in early summer dense, erect spikes of tiny rose-red flowers.

P. amplexicaule (mountain fleece). A long-blooming perennial from the Himalayas, 90 cm (3 ft). Leaves ovate to lanceolate with spikes of bright scarlet flowers from summer to autumn. Varieties include 'Rubrum' and 'Firetail', both rich red.

P. bistorta (snake-weed). A British native, indigenous to damp meadows. Broad basal, dock-like leaves, also in early summer 30–60 cm leafy stems carrying spikes of sessile pale pink flowers. 'Superbum' is an improved variety.

P. campanulatum, Himalayas. A strong grower to 90 cm (3 ft) with elliptic, distinctly veined foliage, dark green above, silvery or buff beneath, and graceful sprays of heather-like white flowers flushed with pink: one of the best. Summer and autumn.

P. cuspidatum, now more correctly *Reynoutria japonica* (Mexican bamboo). A very vigorous Japanese plant which can become weedy. Exploring, rhizomatous roots, stout 2.4 m (8 ft) leafy stems, the leaves elliptic to round and about 125 mm (5 in) long, and panicles of small, greenish-white flowers. A cream-variegated form called 'Spectabile' is less invasive and will grow in deep shade. However, it reverts so must have any green stems regularly removed. Another smaller-growing plant known as 'Compactum' was introduced from Japan about 1935 as *P. reynoutria*. It was said not to spread, which is not my experience, although by regularly pulling out wandering shoots each spring I am able to keep it under control. It has white flowers in late summer which change to pink as they age and are succeeded by red seed pods.

P. vacciniifolium, Himalayas. A short perennial of trailing habit with rounded leaves and racemes of rosy flowers in summer. 30 cm (1 ft).

PRIMULA *(Primulaceae)* primrose

Most primulas require rich, cool and retentive soil, which is continually moist without being sodden. They will not tolerate sourness, the ideal being ground with water lower down, so that the soil above remains damp but sweet. In very acid conditions it may be necessary to add lime, particularly for such species as *P. florindae* and *P. helodoxa*. Primulas, being hungry feeders, need a rich compost so that leafmould or well-decayed farmyard manure with some organic fertilizer, 100 g per sq m (4 oz per sq yd), should be dug into the ground before planting. In later years mulch round the roots with peat or leafsoil to retain the moisture. Propagation of those species mentioned here is by means of seed or spring division. Most belong to the Candelabra group and are moisture-lovers with their flowers arranged in whorls up the stem. Unless otherwise stated they are of Asiatic origin, generally China and Japan, and flower in early summer.

P. aurantiaca grows to 22.5 cm (9 in), with reddish stems and orange-red flowers; the obovate leaves are green with red veins.

P. beesiana, 60 cm (2 ft), fragrant, rosy-carmine flowers around mid-summer; leaves light green, obovate, rough texture.

P. bulleyana, 60–90 cm (2–3 ft). Collected by Forrest in China where it is said to cover vast meadows with its buff-orange flowers; thin, papery leaves. This species also produces variable colour forms.

P. denticulata (drumstick primrose), 30–60 cm (1–2 ft). A plant of robust growth, flowering in early spring with large umbels of pale lavender flowers atop stout, powdery stems, something like drumsticks. The leaves grow in rosettes. Colours vary from white and lavender to deep purple and rich carmine. Good forms can be propagated from root cuttings.

P. florindae (giant cowslip), 90–150 cm (3–5 ft). In wet ground this species attains fine proportions, with clumps of toothed, oblong leaves up to 50 cm (20 in) long. The pendent, fragrant, bell-shaped, citron-yellow flowers, each 18 mm ($\frac{3}{4}$ in) across are borne in large umbels.

P. helodoxa is a candelabra type, 60–90 cm (2–3 ft) high, with whorls of golden yellow flowers.

P. japonica, sometimes called the queen of primroses, is perhaps the showiest and most satisfactory species for the waterside. Although individually some-what short-lived, the plants seed themselves about, producing tier upon tier of pink, white and crimson flowers—many with contrasting 'eyes'—on 60–75 cm (2–2$\frac{1}{2}$ ft) stems. The oblong-ovate leaves grow in rosettes. Selected forms include 'Postford White' and 'Miller's Crimson'.

P. pulverulenta resembles the preceding in general habit but is daintier and further distinguished by its white, mealy stems which carry the whorls of crimson flowers. A varietal group known as the Bartley strain and characterized by buff, apricot, rose-pink and salmon flowers is the one to seek. The early summer flowers of these on their 60–90 cm (2–3 ft) stems are of fairy-like dainti-ness and associate charmingly with blue meconopsis and the soft green fronds of hardy ferns. They bloom in early summer. 'Red Hugh', a variety with orange-red flowers, comes true from seed. 'Inverewe' is another outstanding variety of Scottish origin. A sterile hybrid, it forms rosettes of leaves and has whorls of large orange-scarlet flowers.

P. rosea. A dwarf species, growing a mere 15–23 cm (6–9 in) high, has tufts of toothed leaves and loose umbels of clear rose flowers, borne in heads like polyanthus. The variety 'Delight' ('Visser de Geer') with larger and brighter flowers is slightly taller. This species must have boggy conditions.

P. sikkimensis (Himalayan cowslip), 60 cm (2 ft). A beautiful plant found naturally in the Himalayas from Nepal to Burma and into China in wet, boggy meadows at altitudes of 3300–4500 m (11 000–15 000 ft), where it covers acres of ground with the soft yellow, fragrant, nodding flowers. The long, narrow leaves grow in rosettes. Early summer.

RANUNCULUS *(Ranunculaceae)* buttercup
Most buttercups are natives of moist ground. They are widespread, many of a weedy nature but a few suitable for the bog garden, in sun or light shade. These are propagated by division.

R. aconitifolius, Europe. A vigorous perennial with dark green, palmately divided leaves and masses of single white buttercups on branching stems. 'Flore Pleno' is the best and is commonly known as fair maids of France because, according to Graham Thomas, of its associations with French Huguenot refugees in the 16th century. It has double white blossoms in late spring on 60 cm (2 ft) leafy stems.

R. acris 'Flore Pleno' (yellow bachelor's buttons) flowers at the same time. It is the double form of the European meadow buttercup and originated in Lancashire, England in the 16th century. 45 cm ($1\frac{1}{2}$ ft).

RHEUM *(Polygonaceae)*
Handsome foliage plants of tropical lushness, particularly suitable for semi-wild places or at the margins of water in cool climates. Planted in rich moist soil they can be left to look after themselves to increase annually in beauty. The common edible rhubarb belongs to this genus. Propagated from seed or by division.

R. alexandrae from China is a striking but difficult plant to cultivate. It must have damp soil and a cool climate and atmosphere. Growing about 90 cm (3 ft) tall, it produces strange flower spikes covered for the whole of their length with cream, overlapping bracts which hang down like hundreds of tongues. Early summer.

R. australe (*R. emodi*), Himalayas. A fine foliage plant 1.5–3 m (5–10 ft) in height with wrinkled, broadly ovate leaves and huge plumes of small, dark red flowers in early summer.

R. palmatum, China. A slow-growing plant with gigantic, deeply cut, five-lobed leaves and tall panicles of creamy-white, pink or crimson flowers. Height 2.4–3 m (8–10 ft) at maturity. 'Atrosanguineum' has more deeply dissected leaves, which remain vivid red until such time as the flowers appear, when they become green. The summer flowers are rich crimson borne in great fluffy panicles. *R.p. tanguticum* is a form with less deeply cut leaves, purplish tinted, and crimson flowers.

RODGERSIA *(Saxifragaceae)*
Decorative foliage perennials with thick scaly rhizomes and long feathery panicles of white, cream or pink astilbe-like flowers in summer. They must have a lot of moisture and are often planted in ditches or on stream banks. They also require some shade and are propagated by division in spring or root cuttings.

R. aesculifolia, China, 120 cm (4 ft). A species with bronzed, pinnate leaves, divided like those of the horse chestnut (*Aesculus hippocastanum*), and many branched sprays of small, tightly packed, cream or pink flowers.

R. pinnata, China, 90 cm (3 ft). Pinnately divided, dark olive green or bronzed leaves and plumes of pink flowers, which are brilliant pink in *R.p.* 'Superba'.

R. podophylla, Japan. Known as Rodger's bronze leaf on account of the rich bronzing on the smooth, horse chestnut-like leaves; flowers cream; 90 cm (3 ft).

R. purdomii, China, 60–90 cm (2–3 ft); bronzed palmate foliage, creamy-white flowers.

R. sambucifolia, China, 60–90 cm (2–3 ft); pinnate, bright green leaves; creamy-white flowers.

R. tabularis, now more correctly *Astilboides tabularis*, is quite distinct but nevertheless in spite of its new name looks nothing like an astilbe. It grows about 90 cm (3 ft) high with large, round, green, parasol-like leaves poised on stout stems. These can be 30–90 cm (1–3 ft) across. The flowers are creamy-white in large panicles held well above the foliage.

SANGUISORBA *(Rosaceae)* burnet
Elegant perennials, flowering mid to late summer with long spikes of flowers like slender bottlebrushes and light green, pinnate foliage something like extended rose leaves. All require moist soil and plenty of sun. Propagation by division.

S. canadensis (*Poterium canadense*), N. America. A fine plant for a very wet position growing 90–150 cm (3–5 ft) tall with erect spikes of white flowers. The juice of this plant was formerly used by N. American Indians to stain their faces. It may also be used as a salad plant—having a taste not unlike that of cucumber.

S. obtusa (*Poterium obtusum*) is a fine Japanese species with long, pinnate leaves and arching sprays of brilliant rose, drooping, bottlebrush-like spikes of flowers; 90 cm (3 ft). There is a white-flowered form.

SAXIFRAGA *(Saxifragaceae)*
A large genus, the majority rock plants, easily propagated by seed or division.

S. aquatica (water saxifrage) comes from the high mountains of the Pyrenees, where it frequents marshy ground and streamsides. It is a robust, creeping plant forming thick, 20–23 cm (8–9 in) high cushions of orbicular, three-lobed leaves, above which are carried slender, 30–60 cm (1–2 ft) panicles of white flowers.

S. peltata see *Peltiphyllum*.

SCHIZOSTYLIS *(Iridaceae)* Kaffir lily, crimson flag
Plants resembling small gladioli from warm S. Africa. Notwithstanding this the plants are hardy in southern England and similar warm temperate areas; elsewhere under glass. Their great merit is their late flowering which sometimes extends from early autumn to early winter. Propagation by division.

S. coccinea. Although schizostylis like damp soil they are not aquatics, yet I once saw this species flowering splendidly in waterlogged soil in the late Viscountess Byng's garden at Thorpe in Essex. Certainly it needs humidity and wet at flowering time, also good soil and full sun. The plant makes fibrous, fleshy roots and has several basal, sword-shaped leaves, about 30 cm (1 ft) high and 12 mm (½ in) wide; the crimson-red flowers are borne several to a raceme. There are a number of varieties including 'Viscountess Byng', pale rose-pink, raised by my father-in-law, Amos Perry, in 1939; 'Professor Barnard', dusky pink; 'Mrs Hegarty', pale pink; and 'November Cheer', rosy red.

SCROPHULARIA *(Scrophulariaceae)* figwort
S. aquatica 'Variegata'. Although the species *S. aquatica* is a common and undistinguished European weed, with nettle-like, serrated leaves and small, purplish-brown flowers, the variegated-leaved water figwort is a handsome plant and often grown in damp herbaceous borders as well as bog gardens. The foliage is so heavily splashed with cream it becomes conspicuous at a distance. It is advisable to remove the flower heads as they appear so as to encourage plenty of stocky foliage. Height 60 cm (2 ft). Propagated by division or cuttings.

SEDUM *(Crassulaceae)* stonecrop
S. villosum, from northern Europe, is one of the few species of this extensive genus suitable for bog gardens. Growing 75–100 mm (3–4 in) high it bears small, green leaves and small, pink, long-stalked flowers. It is biennial, found in nature in wet places and by streams where it colonizes from self-set seedlings.

SENECIO *(Compositae)* *(see also* LIGULARIA*)*
S. smithii, S. Chile, Argentina, Falkland Islands. A coarse but unusual perennial for rich damp soil, characterized by large, puckered, horse-radish-like leaves of grey-green, each about 30 cm (1 ft) long, and showy heads made up of many white, yellow-eyed daisies on stout, 90–120 cm (3–4 ft) stems. These are succeeded by fluffy seedheads. It flowers in summer and can be propagated by seed or division.

SIDALCEA *(Malvaceae)*
Although sidalceas are commonly grown in herbaceous borders, they are useful plants for damp—as opposed to wet—positions at the waterside. They make basal clumps of palmately-lobed leaves with leafy-stemmed racemes of satiny, five-petalled flowers—like miniature hollyhocks—in mid to late summer. The stem leaves are cut to the base into narrow segments. Propagated by division.

S. candida, U.S.A. and New Mexico; height 60–90 cm (2–3 ft); buttercup-like leaves and white flowers which age to creamy-yellow.

S. malviflora (checkerbloom). A taller species, up to 120 cm (4 ft), from California with pinkish-rose flowers, the upper leaves lacily segmented. Garden

Lysichiton americanum. A large aroid blooming in early spring before the leaves. Given moist soil or shallow water it increases readily from seed.

Meconopsis betonicifolia. The Himalayan blue poppy usually dies after flowering, but is easily propagated from seed sown immediately after ripening.

forms are usually preferred such as 'Sussex Beauty', clear pink; 'Rev. Page Roberts', soft pink; 'Elsie Heugh', very pale with fringed petals; 'Nimmerdor', crimson-purple; and 'Oberon', clear pink.

SMILACINA *(Liliaceae)* false Solomon's seal
Handsome plants with feathery panicles of spiraea-like flowers and lily-of-the-valley foliage on long arching stems. They prefer a rich, moist, partially shaded position. Propagated by seed or division.

S. racemosa, N. America. A plant with the growth habit of Solomon's seal (*Polygonatum multiflorum*), to which it is related, the leafy stems about 90 cm (3 ft) long, topped by 15 cm (6 in) inflorescences of fluffy white or pinkish, small flowers. These are succeeded by red berries.

SOLIDAGO *(Compositae)* golden rod
A coarse but useful genus of autumn-flowering perennials, which are frequently a nuisance in the U.S.A. but welcomed in Britain and northern Europe. Garden cultivars from *S. virgaurea*, like 'Goldenmosa' with tight balls of yellow flowers 75 cm (2½ ft) tall, 'Lemore' soft primrose 60 cm (2 ft) and 'Cloth of Gold' 45 cm (1½ ft), are popular in Europe and if they can be induced to spread in moist, sunny situations are very striking. Propagate by division.

SYMPHYTUM *(Boraginaceae)* comfrey
Rough-foliaged plants with tubular, usually pendent flowers in scorpioid cymes. These uncurl like a watch-spring as the blooms develop. The species, natives of Europe and western Asia, are decorative in spring and early summer and make good plants for damp soil, preferably in light shade. They are propagated by division or root cuttings.

S. caucasicum, Caucasus. Leaves ovate lanceolate, hairy on both sides; flowers reddish-purple when young, developing to azure blue, in pendent clusters; 60 cm (2 ft).

S. × uplandicum (Russian comfrey) is a coarse, leafy plant, up to 120 cm (4 ft) with thick roots, large, hairy, oblong leaves and pink-budded flowers which open pale blue in late spring and early summer. 'Variegatum' has cream leaf splashes and variegations, and pale pink flowers. It is inclined to revert to plain green so must be checked occasionally.

SYMPLOCARPUS *(Araceae)* skunk cabbage, polecat weed
S. foetidus. A curious N. American plant for partial shade, having a foetid odour when bruised, similar to that of a skunk. The hooded, 75–150 mm (3–6 in) spathes usually grow in clumps and show a wide colour range, being mottled with purple and yellowish-green, changing in part to crimson, dark green and yellow. They appear very early in the spring, several weeks before the leaves, which are large and oval cordate to 45 cm long and 30 cm wide.

THALICTRUM *(Ranunculaceae)* meadow rue
Plants mainly with fibrous roots (although a few have tuberous rootstocks), leaves many times divided into numerous leaflets and branching stems with many dainty flowers. A few are suitable for the bog garden. These need rich moist soil, which does not become waterlogged, and light shade. Those mentioned here are propagated by seed or division.

   T. aquilegifolium, Europe, northern Asia. A variable plant of 60–90 cm (2–3 ft) with slender, glaucous stems, deeply lobed leaves and fluffy, usually purple stamened flowers on spreading panicles in early summer. White, deep purple, pale and rosy forms are available.

   T. chelidonii, a Himalayan plant for cool, moist, peaty soil, which will not dry out in summer. It grows 90–120 cm (3–4 ft) high with dainty, compound, many-lobed, smooth leaves with loose panicles of 25 mm (1 in) wide, mauve-sepalled flowers filled with showy yellow stamens. Propagated by seed or division.

   T. delavayi, W. China, 60–150 cm (2–5 ft). One of the finest with large and many mauve flowers on cobweb fine stems. 'Hewitt's Double' has double flowers like the French knots in needlework. It blooms in summer and has its leaves divided like those of maidenhair ferns.

   T. flavum glaucum (*T. speciossimum*), Spain. Grows 60–150 cm (2–5 ft) tall with glaucous, divided leaves and erect pyramids of fluffy, yellow flowers in mid-summer.

TRADESCANTIA *(Commelinaceae)* spiderwort
T. × andersoniana. A race of hybrids from *T. virginiana* and other species, easily grown in most soils—dry or moist, in sun or partial shade. All have lax, long, narrow leaves like those of bluebells and throughout the summer many three-petalled flowers in umbels. These have showy, very hairy stamens. Cultivars of merit include 'Osprey', large white with blue stamens; 'J. C. Weguelin', pale blue; 'Isis', deep blue; 'Purple Dome', purple; 'Iris Prichard', white and bright blue; and 'Purewell Giant', carmine. Propagated by division.

TRILLIUM *(Liliaceae)* wake robin, Trinity flower, wood lily
Spring-flowering, woodland plants which need light shade and cool, moist soil. They should be planted about 5 cm (2 in) deep, in groups. The plants have short, thick rootstocks, and each stem bears three leaves, three calyces, three petals and twice-three (six) stamens; hence the name Trinity flower. All are N. American natives, propagated by seed or division. About a dozen species are grown by connoisseurs in Europe; some very rare. The most readily available and likely to succeed in gardens are the following.

   T. cernuum (nodding trillium) nodding, white, narrow-petalled flowers on 30 mm ($1\frac{1}{4}$ in) stems, beneath trifoliate leaves, the leaflets of which are oval and each about 10 cm (4 in) long, overall height 30–45 cm (1–$1\frac{1}{2}$ ft).

T. chloropetalum, leaflets larger than preceding, to 15 cm (6 in), and often mottled with grey. Flowers 9 cm ($3\frac{1}{2}$ in) long but very variable in colour, from white or greenish-yellow to crimson-maroon; 60 cm (2 ft).

T. erectum (squawroot, stinking Benjamin, lamb's quarters). An evil-smelling species whose white, fleshy roots have medicinal uses; tannin and bitter extract are also derived from them. The 5 cm (2 in), sessile flowers are usually reddish-purple, but white or yellowish forms occur occasionally like *albiflorum* (var. *album*) and 'Ochroleucum'. 45–60 cm ($1\frac{1}{2}$–2 ft).

T. grandiflorum (wake robin). The largest-flowered member of the genus, with pure white blooms, up to 75 mm (3 in) across, which fade with age to rosy-pink. A double called 'Flore Pleno' is particularly outstanding. 45 cm.

T. sessile (toadshade) is the first to flower and distinct on account of its mottled leaves, which are green heavily blotched with maroon, grey and white. The flowers are stalkless, maroon-purple, 35 mm ($1\frac{1}{2}$ in) long. Height 30 cm.

TROLLIUS *(Ranunculaceae)* globe flower
Moisture-loving perennials related to buttercups, ideal for bog gardens and the margins of streams. They have fibrous roots, basal, deeply divided or lobed leaves and in spring and early summer large, round, buttercup-like flowers on leafy stems. The petals are usually incurved to make globe-shaped blooms. They must never become dry at the roots and are propagated by seed or division.

The best for garden use are varieties from the European *T. europaeus* and various Chinese species. They include 'Orange Princess', orange-gold; 'Wargrave Variety', bright yellow; 'Canary Bird', lemon-yellow; 'Earliest of All', light yellow; and 'Golden Queen', rich gold. All grow about 60 cm (2 ft) tall.

UVULARIA *(Liliaceae)* merrybells
A small genus of rhizomatous perennials from N. America, which flower in early spring and thrive in damp vegetative soil in light shade. They have leafy stems, the blades a light delicate green and perfoliate, also numerous drooping, campanulate, yellow flowers with six segments. Propagated by division.

U. grandiflora, flowers lemon-yellow, about 5 cm (2 in) long; leaves oblong or oblong lanceolate, 125 mm (5 in) in length; 60 cm (2 ft). 'Pallida' has paler flowers and only grows to 38 cm (15 in).

U. perfoliata. Rather smaller than preceding; leaves 9 cm ($3\frac{1}{2}$ in); flowers 3 cm ($1\frac{1}{4}$ in), pale yellow; 45 cm ($1\frac{1}{2}$ ft).

U. sessiliflora. Flowers very narrow, greenish-yellow, 3 cm ($1\frac{1}{4}$ in) long; the leaves sessile but not perfoliate; 30 cm (1 ft).

VERATRUM *(Liliaceae)* false helleborine
Stately plants for deep, moist soil in sun or partial shade, capable of standing alone as accent plants in key situations. The large, handsome leaves are pleated; the flowers small but many in broad, branching racemes. The thick rhizomes

have various medicinal uses and are poisonous. Propagation by seed or division.

V. *album* is European with greenish-white flowers on 1.8 m (6 ft) stems; V. *nigrum*, also European, has maroon-purple flowers, 1.8 m (6 ft); V. *viride*, N. America, grows 1.2 m (4 ft) with starry, green flowers. This is perhaps the most striking and is known as Indian poke. All bloom in summer.

VIOLA *(Violaceae)*

A few violets grow naturally in moist soil and can be naturalized in open spots beneath shrubs. They need little care after planting and generally spread naturally from seeds or runners.

V. *canina* (dog violet), northern Europe and Asia. A British plant which may be planted for the beauty of its scentless, blue flowers in early spring. Leaves rounded, toothed. 75–100 mm (3–4 in).

V. *palustris* (marsh violet), N. America, Europe, Asia. A creeping plant with round, wavy, toothed leaves and pale lilac flowers streaked with violet-blue, 12 mm ($\frac{1}{2}$ in) across.

V. *renifolia*, N. American swamps. Large, kidney-shaped leaves, 10 cm (4 in) across; flowers white with brown veins.

WATSONIA *(Iridaceae)* bugle lily

Watsonias are tall, 90–150 cm (3–5 ft), S. African plants which grow from corms planted 12 cm (5 in) deep, and they greatly resemble gladioli. In Britain they are hardy only in warm, sheltered places, whereas in parts of western Australia they grow along river courses and streams and have become almost a weed. In frost-prone places the corms can be lifted and stored like gladioli.

W. *pyramidata* (W. *rosea*) has 75 cm (2$\frac{1}{2}$ ft) long, 25 mm (1 in) wide, strap-shaped leaves in summer, strong 120–150 cm (4–5 ft) stems carrying clear rose-pink, funnel-shaped flowers, each about 75 mm (3 in) long on one side of the spikes. There is also a white form. Propagated by seed or by offsets or cormlets.

ZANTEDESCHIA *(Araceae)* calla lily, arum lily

Well-known S. African plants at one time much forced in greenhouses in Europe.

Z. *aethiopica* is the hardiest species and forms of it will grow outside in the southern counties of England and areas with similar climate. One called 'Crowborough', which is almost identical with the type species, has been growing in our garden for over 20 years without protection and has also seeded itself about. Full sun and dry soil during the dormant period is the secret of success and laying a sheet of glass or some plastic sheeting over the roots or a mulch of dry leaves should help it establish. This form has glossy, arrow-shaped leaves, about 30 cm (1 ft) long and 15 cm (6 in) wide on long, smooth stems and 12–15 cm (5–6 in) pure white flowers with a deep golden, poker-like spadix in each. They bloom all summer and should be propagated from seed.

11

Other plants for bog gardens
and damp situations

Trees and shrubs

ACER *(Aceraceae)* maple
Handsome trees and shrubs with large, mostly hand-shaped leaves which are deciduous and often show fine autumnal tints prior to falling. A few will grow in wet swampy soil.

A. rubrum (swamp or red maple), grows eventually to 21 m (70 ft) or more, forming a rounded head of branches. In its native N. America the three or five lobed leaves become brilliant scarlet and orange in autumn; rather less so in northern Europe. The rich red flowers appear before the leaves in early spring.

A. saccharinum (silver maple), another N. American, grows around 30 m (100 ft) high with greenish-yellow flowers and five-lobed leaves which turn yellow in autumn.

ALNUS *(Betulaceae)* alder
Most alders appreciate wet, swampy positions, too moist even for willows, and are planted for the beauty of the male catkins in spring and for the wood, which is extremely durable in water. It was formerly much used for boats and bridge piles, including, according to historians, the famous Rialto bridge in Venice. The bark of the young tree is a powerful astringent and the catkins produce a dye, while the split roots may be fashioned into baskets. The tree is often planted to hold up river banks. The species may be propagated from seed; cultivars grafted on stock of suitable species.

Good kinds for the garden include *A. glutinosa*, the common European form and its cultivars with variously shaped or golden leaves as in 'Aurea'. It normally grows 15–24 m (50–90 ft) with dull green, almost round leaves.

A. japonica, Japan. Normally prefers a drier position but is a fine handsome tree 15–23 m (50–80 ft) tall, of pyramidal habit with dark green oval leaves, small black cone-like fruits, and erect male catkins.

ANDROMEDA *(Ericaceae)*
A. polifolia (bog rosemary), a low evergreen shrub from northern Europe and northern Asia. It rarely grows more than 45 cm (18 in) high, the wiry stems thickly packed with stiff narrow leaves, felted beneath, and compact clusters of pink, pitcher-shaped flowers in early summer. It is commonly found in sphagnum peat bogs and dislikes lime. Propagated by cuttings or seed.

ARCTOSTAPHYLOS *(Ericaceae)* bearberry
Handsome evergreen shrubs for acid soils, mostly confined to western N. America. The leaves are leathery, the flowers urn-shaped, borne in short racemes. They are succeeded by fleshy, rounded fruits. Usually propagated from cuttings or seeds.

   A. manzanita, the manzanita from California, with deep pink flowers and orange berries, needs sun, but the commonest in gardens is *A. uva-ursi*, the bearberry, a trailing shrub with long slender branches, small, tapering obovate leaves and white or pink flowers in early spring. Northern hemisphere.

BETULA *(Betulaceae)* birch
Although most birches need well drained loamy soil, there are a few tolerant of bog conditions or places with a high water table. The elegant pendulous branches, at times hung with dainty catkins, carry small bright leaves which are rarely attacked by insects. Even in winter the erect, silvery trunks add a touch of colour to the landscape. They are best raised from seed.

   The best species for the bog garden are *B. nana* which only grows 60–120 cm (2–4 ft) high and comes from arctic N. America, Europe and Asia; *B. nigra*, (river birch), 15 m (50 ft), with flanking, dark bark, N. American; and *B. pubescens* (downy birch), from northern Asia and Europe, a tree to 21 m (70 ft) with peeling white bark which is dark near the base. Its varieties include forms with yellow leaves and dwarfs. A fragrant oil is obtained from the wood, used in the making of Russian leather.

CLETHRA *(Clethraceae)*
C. alnifolia (sweet pepper-bush). A deciduous N. American shrub for moist peaty soils, 2.5–2.75 m (8–9 ft) high, with erect branches, obovate leaves and racemes of fragrant white flowers. Propagated by seeds or sucker growths.

CORNUS *(Cornaceae)* cornel, dogwood
Dogwoods are decorative at all seasons. A few are conspicuous on account of their variegated foliage or handsome spring flowers. Some are noted for their richly coloured fruits and there are others with brilliant red or yellow barked stems, which bring colour to the winter landscape. As most grow equally well in sun or shade and flourish in most soils their value is enhanced. In early spring coloured stemmed varieties should be cut hard back after flowering to encourage

this feature, for it is the young wood which shows the most vivid colouration. Propagated by seed, cuttings, layers or with the flowering varieties by budding or grafting.

C. *alba*, Siberia and China. Produces a thicket of stems with blood-red branches, oval pointed leaves, flattened heads of small yellowish-white flowers and bluish-white oval fruits. There are forms with variegated foliage, especially 'Spaethii', gold-splashed, and 'Elegantissima', creamy-white. The species is specially recommended for the banks of a pond or stream.

C. *stolonifera* from N. America is closely related to the preceding and is a vigorous shrub up to 2.5 m (8 ft) with purplish-red branches, white flowers and white fruits. The variety 'Flaviramea' has yellow branches, which look attractive all winter.

DECODON (*see* p. 60)

GAULTHERIA *(Ericaceae)*
G. *procumbens* (creeping wintergreen) is a dwarf evergreen 5–15 cm (2–6 in) high, useful for ground cover on moist soil, with aromatic, glossy, oval leaves and solitary white flowers succeeded by scarlet berries. An oil extracted from these is used in perfumery and medicine, and because partridges greedily consume the fruits it is also known as partridge berry. It comes from Canada and may be propagated by layers, seeds or division.

HYDRANGEA *(Hydrangeaceae)*
Well known shrubs which, since they resent dryness at the roots, are ideal for moist soil in the bog garden. They look particularly attractive planted close to water so that the flowers are reflected in still pools or lakes. They are not winter hardy in very severe climates so should be given sheltered situations, or else grown in pots which can be plunged to their rims outside in late spring and mulched with moist peat and brought under cover for winter.

Alternatively, they look very well in tubs stood at vantage points at the edges of formal pools. Propagation is by cuttings, or layers for some species. Garden varieties from the Japanese H. *macrophylla* are the most useful, particularly the round-headed, sterile flowered Hortensias and also the charming Lacecaps. The latter have fertile flowers in the centre, fringed with rings of sterile blooms. Blue colouring is dependent on the concentration of aluminium ions in the soil water—dictated by the degree of acidity in the soil. The best blues—like 'Blue Wave' (Lacecap) and 'Europa', 'Westfalen' and 'Parsifal' (Hortensias) are superb on acid soils. There are also whites in both sections and pinks and reds which do best under alkaline conditions. All have a long summer season.

KALMIA *(Ericaceae)* sheep laurel, calico bush
Kalmias need moist peaty soil and grow very well in swampy places if planted

Kalmia latifolia

on low mounds. They are medium or low shrubs with oblong leaves (said to be poisonous to animals) and terminal clusters of showy, saucer-shaped, white, rosy-red or pink flowers. They dislike lime. Propagated by seed, layers or half-ripe cuttings in August.

K. *latifolia* from the eastern U.S.A. is probably the best; a robust evergreen, it makes a dense thicket 3 m (10 ft) or so high and more across with large glossy leaves and in early summer white to deep rose flowers the shape of an inverted sunshade.

K. *polifolia*, also N. American, grows naturally in bogs, but is shorter at 30–60 cm (1–2 ft) with pale purplish flowers in spring.

LIQUIDAMBAR (*Hamamelidaceae*)

L. *styraciflua* (sweet gum). A beautiful deciduous tree from Honduras and Guatemala, also the eastern U.S.A., where it is often found growing in swamps. Although taller in the wild it rarely exceeds 18 m (60 ft) in Europe and has large maple-like, palmate leaves on long stalks. It is at its best in autumn when the tree appears to be on fire, so vivid are the autumnal tints, scarlet, purple, crimson, orange and even green leaves, all on the same tree. The tree produces a fragrant resin, called American oil of styrax or storax, which is used for scenting soaps and the like. The hard and heavy wood is often called 'satin walnut' and used for furniture, cabinet work, etc. It is usually propagated from seed, which gives variable results, or layers.

METASEQUOIA *(Taxodiaceae)*
M. glyptostroboides (water fir, dawn redwood). The strange history of this Chinese, deciduous conifer is well known. Although common in prehistoric times and discovered in many places in a fossil state, living trees were not found until 1941. It has proved hardy in Britain and many other countries and since it reproduces easily from half ripe summer cuttings is now widespread. It was found in wet ravines and along stream banks in China, and given similar conditions grows rapidly, eventually making a tree up to 30 m (100 ft) with handsome light green leaves, deeply cut into narrow linear segments. These turn rosy-brown in autumn prior to leaf-fall. Grown in dryish conditions, it develops much more slowly but makes a better balanced tree. Our own specimen, planted in 1948 on gravelly soil, is in 1980 about 6 m (20 ft) high, but very compact with branches right down to ground level.

MYRICA *(Myricaceae)* bog myrtle, bayberry, wax myrtle
Fragrant foliaged shrubs with inconspicuous flowers and a wax round the fruits which has been used in the manufacture of slow-burning, aromatic candles. The root bark is astringent and also the leaves of some species like *M. gale*, which have medicinal uses. *M. gale* is propagated by suckers, others by seed or layers.

M. gale (sweet gale) has a wide distribution in the northern hemisphere, its leaves similar to but smaller than *M. pensylvanica*. These are fragrant when bruised, and in Yorkshire in England were once used for flavouring beer. The stiff golden catkins of the male plant appear in summer, those of the female usually on a separate plant.

M. pensylvanica (*M. cerifera*) (wax myrtle) is an evergreen shrub with narrow, obovate leaves around 7.5 cm (3 in) long and 2 cm ($\frac{3}{4}$ in) wide. N. America.

OXYCOCCUS *(Ericaceae)* cranberry
O. macrocarpus is the American cranberry, much cultivated in the U.S.A. for its edible fruit. It is of creeping habit bearing oval, evergreen leaves which are whitish beneath, pink summer flowers and round, red berries.

O. palustris from northern and central Europe, northern Asia and N. America grows wild in the British Isles. At one time the berries were avidly gathered but drainage of the wet boggy areas where the plant once thrived has destroyed much of their old habitat. The species is similar to but with smaller berries than *O. macrocarpus*. An acid soil is essential. Propagated from seed or cuttings.

PERNETTYA *(Ericaceae)*
P. mucronata is an evergreen shrub from Chile noteworthy on account of its

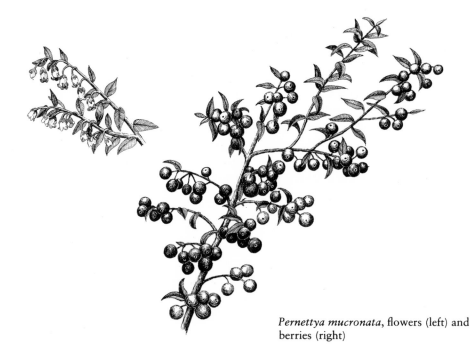

Pernettya mucronata, flowers (left) and berries (right)

large, marble-sized berries which come in a variety of shades from white to pink, crimson, magenta, purple and near black. Male and female flowers appear on separate bushes so it is necessary to have at least one male plant for five or six females. The bushes grow 0.7–1.5 m (2–5 ft) tall, with dense but very narrow, spiny-pointed leaves and small nodding white flowers in early summer. It is a very hardy plant, favouring moist, acid soils; its berries maintain their colour through autumn and winter. Propagated from seed.

SALIX *(Salicaceae)* willow, osier

Willows have a natural affinity with water and perhaps no trees are more suitable for waterside plantings. They thrive in most soils provided they are constantly moist, and vary from alpine species, only a few inches high, to tall elegant trees. In addition to their decorative qualities willows are often used to fix river banks against erosion.

The young pliant stems of osiers make excellent basket material and have been used for this purpose since earliest times; ancient Britons skilfully weaved the light material into boats (coracles). The wood is soft and easy to split and bend, that of some species being used for cricket bats, wooden clogs, artificial limbs, furniture and the like. The charcoal makes gunpowder and the leaves and bark are the source of dyes and even have medicinal properties. The sexes are usually on separate plants and all species and cultivars root readily from cuttings. In the water garden weeping willows are usually the most popular, especially forms of *S. babylonica*, presumably originating in China although this is not certain. It grows to 9 m (30 ft) with long, drooping branches, carrying narrowly lanceolate leaves about 15 cm (6 in) in length and greenish catkins. Cultivars include 'Aurea' with golden branches and 'Crispa' which has twisted curled leaves.

S. caprea is the common pussy willow whose golden male catkins are so familiar in spring. It grows to 6 m (20 ft) and in England is known as 'palm', an allusion to its use in churches on Palm Sunday. There is a weeping form called 'Pendula' or the Kilmarnock willow, but perhaps the most attractive of all are derivatives of the white willow, *S. alba*, a widespread species in the northern hemisphere. This is the cricket bat willow; 'Tristis' has bright yellow drooping branches and *S.c.* var. *vitellina* golden branches and leaves which are glaucous underneath. *S. × blanda*, known as the Wisconsin weeping willow, is popular in the U.S.A.

SORBARIA *(Rosaceae)*
A group of shrubs similar to spiraea but with pinnate instead of simple leaves. All are vigorous plants which do well near water and all have heavy plumes of white or creamy flowers in late summer and early autumn.

S. aitchisonii (*Spiraea aitchisonii*) from Afghanistan and Kashmir. Grows 1.75–2.5 m (6–8 ft); the young upright stems are often bright red and bear large, cone-shaped panicles of white flowers in late summer.

S. arborea from China is similar but taller, 3–6 m (10–20 ft).

SPIRAEA *(Rosaceae)*
A genus of easily grown and ornamental deciduous shrubs for the waterside with plumes of white, pink, cream or crimson flowers in spring and summer. They should be planted in a moist, sunny spot but are not particular as to soil. Propagation by division or suckers.

S. × arguta, the bridal wreath, is a spring-flowering hybrid of garden origin growing 1–2 m (3–6 ft) high with 2.5 cm (1 in), oblong ovate leaves and small umbels of white flowers all down the branches. *S. × bumalda* is another good hybrid with white to deep pink, large, terminal sprays of flowers and has a variety 'Anthony Waterer', bright crimson, which also has red young growths; and 'Ruberrima', rosy-red. *S. japonica* is a Japanese species 1.25–2 m (4–6 ft) high with coarsely toothed, lanceolate-ovate leaves and large sprays of pink flowers. It has many cultivars, like the dark red 'Atrosanguinea'.

TAXODIUM *(Taxodiaceae)* bog cypress, bald cypress, swamp cypress
T. distichum is native to the southern U.S.A. and closely resembles metasequoia (p. 151). A handsome deciduous tree of pyramidal habit, it will grow 30 m

(100 ft) or more with buttressed trunks and in wet places makes root projections called 'knees', which extend above the water and enable the roots to breathe. The deeply divided leaves colour an attractive shade of reddish-brown before falling in autumn. Male and female flowers are separate but on the same tree. *T. ascendens nutans* is a weeping form. Taxodiums are excellent for low swampy places and are propagated from seeds or cuttings.

VACCINIUM *(Ericaceae)* blueberry

A large genus of shrubs, mostly inhabitants of acid and peaty bogs, which do not care for lime and often will not grow in rich soil. Many have edible fruits and attractive autumnal tints.

V. myrtilloides, from northern and central Europe and northern Asia, has a number of popular names like bilberry, whortleberry, whinberry and blueberry. It has deciduous, thin, ovate, finely toothed leaves about 2.5 cm (1 in) long; globular, greenish-pink flowers and black, glaucous fruits. These can be eaten fresh or cooked, also used for wine (to give it colour), syrups and sauces.

V. vitis-idaea, variously known as cowberry, foxberry, or mountain cranberry, is a low, evergreen, creeping shrub, 15–25 cm (6–10 in) tall, with wiry stems covered when young with black down. It has neat leaves like box, 3.5 cm ($1\frac{1}{4}$ in) in length, white or rose, bell-shaped flowers and acid, dark red fruits, sometimes used as a substitute for true cranberries (*V. macrocarpon*).

Bulbs for the bog garden

LEUCOJUM *(Amaryllidaceae)* snowflake

Certain snowflakes are most at home in damp places where, if left alone, they increase and naturalize. At Myddelton House, Enfield, they romp over a wet meadow, where they associate happily with calthas and other bog plants.

L. vernum (spring snowflake), from central Europe, has narrow grassy leaves and pendent, white, green-tipped bells which are fragrant. Height 15 cm (6 in) but up to 60 cm (2 ft) in the superior, robust form called 'Vagneri'.

L. aestivum (summer snowflake or Loddon lily, which grows in England near the river Loddon) belies its name for it is still a spring bloomer although later than preceding. The variety 'Gravetye Giant' is an outstanding plant, 60 cm (2 ft) tall with robust stems, green narrow leaves and clusters of white flowers, green-tipped with six segments. Propagated by seed or offsets.

LILIUM *(Liliaceae)* lily

Among the large family of lilies are several which favour damp conditions, particularly in moist, peaty yet well-drained soils. *L. canadense* (Canadian lily), widespread in certain N. American States, was the first lily brought to Britain from that continent. Growing $1–1\frac{1}{2}$ m (3–5 ft) tall with whorls of lanceolate leaves down the stems, the nodding, bell-shaped flowers come in summer and are bright orange-yellow with recurved petals, spotted inside with brown. The bulbs have creeping stolons so that the plants spread if left alone. *L. pardalinum*, the leopard lily of California, has scentless, orange-red to crimson, brown spotted, Turk's cap flowers atop 1.25–1.75 m (4–7 ft) leafy stems, the latter arranged in whorls. Summer blooming, it is suitable for any moist but not water logged position, in full sun. *L. superbum*, the swamp lily of N. America, favours moist slopes, acid meadows and marshes. Growing 1–2.5 m (3–8 ft) high, the purplish stems carry many maroon spotted, brilliant orange flowers, 7.5–10 cm (3–4 in) across in late summer. Plant the bulbs 13–23 cm (5–9 in) deep, setting them on a few stones to prevent standing water, but avoid lime. Propagated by seed or offsets.

NARCISSUS (*Amaryllidaceae*) daffodil, narcissus
In the Pyrenees many narcissi grow in alpine meadows which are subject to

Lilium superbum

flooding as the early snows melt. Accordingly such plants are useful early bloomers in open spaces along the margins of lakes and streams or between perennial bog plants. If left alone to naturalize, species like the 25–30 cm (10–12 in) *N. pseudonarcissus*, the fragrant wild daffodil of western Europe (including Britain), *N. bulbocodium* of S. France, the 10–15 cm (4–6 in) hoop petticoat, and *N. cyclamineus*, now more correctly *Corbularia bulbocodium*, from Portugal, which grows about the same height, form broad colonies which are a delight each spring. Propagation is by seed or offsets.

Ground cover plants for damp situations

AJUGA *(Labiatae)* bugleweed

Annuals and perennials, belonging to north temperate regions of the Old World. They reproduce vegetatively by means of runners, most rapidly in moist heavy soils, and thrive in sun or light shade. The small, sage-like flowers appear on basal spikes in spring or early summer. They make good carpeters, the coloured-leafed forms being particularly attractive.

A. genevensis, Europe and Asia. Small, dark green, oblong leaves, on rhizomatous stems and 15–23 cm (6–9 in) erect spikes of bright blue, rarely white or pink, flowers. There is also a variegated cream and green leafed form.

A. reptans, the common bugle of English woodlands and its coloured-leafed forms are the most popular for gardens. All have bright blue flowers on leafy stems. The plants are stoloniferous with ovate basal leaves about 5 cm (2 in) long and 25 mm (1 in) wide, plain green in the type, but cream variegated in 'Variegata', purplish in 'Atropurpurea' and red, white, yellow and green in 'Multicolor'. 'Alba' has white flowers, 'Rosea' pink, and 'Rubra' purplish-red.

ANAGALLIS *(Primulaceae)* pimpernel

A. tenella (bog pimpernel). A British native of marshy areas, making prostrate mats of tiny, simple leaves spangled with almost stemless, clear pink, honey-scented, five-petalled flowers. Full sun.

A. monelli, southern Europe. This has blue flowers, gentian-blue in the cultivar 'Phillipsii', which grows to 30 cm (1 ft), with trailing, rather woody stems. Propagated by division.

CHRYSOSPLENIUM *(Saxifragaceae)* golden saxifrage

Small, semi-aquatic, creeping plants for carpeting wet, muddy places in bog gardens. Propagated by division.

C. alternifolium, Europe and northern Asia, grows to 15 cm (6 in) with alternate, rounded, toothed leaves and small greenish flowers in early spring.

C. americanum (water carpet), N. American. A smooth, creeping species with ovate to rounded, small leaves and yellow-green flowers; spring.

C. oppositifolium. A European species growing some 15 cm (6 in) high with abundant, bright green, orbicular leaves and clusters of yellowish-green, very small, four-sepalled flowers in late spring.

CORNUS *(Cornaceae)*
C. canadensis (Chamaepericlymenum canadense) (bunchberry, dwarf cornel, crackerberry). A beautiful little N. American woodland plant, forming carpets of ovate to elliptic, leathery, dark green leaves which are spangled in spring with tight heads of showy white small flowers surrounded by involucres of four to six, large, white, petal-like bracts on 7.5–22 cm (3–9 in) stems. These are succeeded by bright red berries in autumn. The plants must have cool soil, with light shade and no lime. Propagation by division.

C. *suecica* from arctic Europe and Asia also has white flowers and scarlet berries. It grows a few inches high but is usually more difficult to establish than preceding.

EPIGAEA *(Ericaceae)* ground laurel
Creeping evergreens for shady, moist, acid soil. They detest lime and disturbance so are often difficult to establish, seed sown immediately after harvesting proving a more satisfactory method of propagation than division.

E. asiatica from Japan has prostrate hairy stems, rooting into the ground, round leathery leaves and terminal or axillary clusters of rose flowers.

E. repens (trailing arbutus, mayflower), N. America. Oblong ovate, bright green, leathery leaves about 7.5 cm (3 in) in length and fragrant, salver-shaped, pink to white flowers in spring. A decoction of the leaves was formerly used as a tonic by N. American Indians. The species has slightly fragrant, five-lobed blooms in terminal, rarely axillary clusters. It requires more shade than *E. asiatica* and was introduced to Britain in 1736.

LYSIMACHIA *(Primulaceae)*
L. nummularia (moneywort, creeping Jenny, creeping Charlie, herb-twopence). Most lysimachias are upright plants, some quite tall, but this European species is a real carpeter. At the pool's edge it will also creep into the water from damp soil and is also used by aquarists in aquaria. Its long trailing stems are well clothed with smooth, green, opposite, nearly round leaves, 12–25 mm ($\frac{1}{2}$–1 in) long with axillary, solitary, bright golden, cup-shaped flowers in early summer. 'Aurea' has yellow leaves, and is just as floriferous, so is a better plant for gardens. The leaves have been used to seal wounds and also to make tea. Propagation by division.

MITCHELLA *(Rubiaceae)*
M. repens (partridge berry, running box, squawberry, twinberry). An evergreen trailer from N. America and eastern Asia, suitable for damp, shady places. It

has tiny, opposite, rounded, dark green leaves, to 18 mm ($\frac{3}{4}$ in), which are glossy above, often veined in white, carried on 30 cm (1 ft) rooting stems. The fragrant white flowers come in axillary or terminal pairs and are succeeded by red (rarely white) twin berries. The leaves have medicinal properties. Propagated by division.

NARTHECIUM *(Liliaceae)* bog asphodel

N. ossifragum is often found in Europe with its feet in water, amongst tufts of grass and sphagnum. It grows 15–20 cm (6–8 in) tall with tufts of leaves like miniature iris foliage, the spikes of rich yellow, six-parted flowers in upright racemes. Since sheep pasturing in wet boggy places are often liable to foot rot, it was once believed that this disease was due to their grazing on bog asphodel. Hence this innocent plant received the name *ossifragum*, i.e. 'bone breaker'.

Several N. American species are taller like *N. americanum*, 45 cm (1$\frac{1}{2}$ ft); *N. californicum*, 30 cm (1 ft); also the Japanese *N. asiaticum*, 60 cm (2 ft). All are found in wet places, have yellow flowers and are propagated by division.

Ferns for the bog garden

Most ferns will grow in moist shade but the following are particularly good near water, especially the hart's tongues which will even peep out beneath dripping waterfalls, and the tall osmundas which thrive in shallow water. Nevertheless ferns should never be planted in direct drips—from buildings or trees—as these spoil the foliage. Most prefer an acid soil and appreciate annual top-dressings of peat or leaf soil. They are propagated from spores (a slow process) or division during the resting period.

ASPLENIUM *(Aspleniaceae)*

A. scolopendrium (Phyllitis scolopendrium; Scolopendrium vulgare) (hart's tongue fern), N. hemisphere. Rich green, broad, strap-shaped leaves, all basal and evergreen. There are countless variants with crisped, frilled, crested and curled margins, also branched or twisted leaves. Usual height around 30 cm.

ATHYRIUM *(Athyriaceae)*

A. filix-femina (lady fern), cosmopolitan. A pretty fern growing to 60 cm (2 ft) with finely cut, vivid green fronds of fairy-like daintiness. It is deciduous and at its best in early spring.

A. goeringianum 'Pictum' (Japanese painted fern) is distinct because of its leaf colouration, the stems being maroon-red and the fronds green with grey central stripes. 60 cm (2 ft). It needs a sheltered spot.

MATTEUCCIA *(Onocleaceae)*

M. struthiopteris (Struthiopteris germanica; Onoclea struthiopteris) (ostrich plume fern), northern hemisphere. Very graceful plant with erect, pale green,

Mimulus × *burnetii*. A hybrid musk with the habit of *M. luteus*. It has copper-yellow flowers, spotted with brown and yellow throats.

Primula 'Inverewe' and *Rodgersia aesculifolia*. Good companions at the waterside, the primula a showy candelabra with large orange-scarlet flowers and the rodgersia with bronzed horse chestnut-like leaves.

deciduous fronds about 1 m ($3\frac{1}{4}$ ft) long, arranged in a circle so that they resemble giant shuttlecocks. Grow in shade and perennially moist or boggy soil.

ONOCLEA *(Onocleaceae)*
O. sensibilis (sensitive fern). A highly adaptable N. American fern. It can be successfully grown in fairly dry, shady areas but for best results should be planted near water, in sun or shade, when it will ramble in and out of the water to form dense carpets. Deciduous.

OSMUNDA *(Osmundaceae)*
O. cinnamomea (cinnamon fern), N. America, has light green fronds up to 1.2 m (4 ft). When young and furled these are covered with cinnamon-brown woolly fluff. Deciduous.

  O. claytoniana, N. America. Commonly called the interrupted fern because the fertile fronds of brown pinnae have a bare spot or interruption in the middle. 1 m (3 ft), deciduous.

  O. regalis (royal fern, flowering fern), cosmopolitan. The handsomest species with fine sterile fronds up to 1.2–1.5 m (4–5 ft), pale green in spring but turning russet brown in autumn. The fertile fronds rise on separate stalks and look like green and brown flowers—hence one of its common names. The young furled fronds are edible. Deciduous.

WOODWARDIA *(Blechnaceae)*
W. areolata (chain fern), N. America. Likes a wet, swampy soil and grows 30 cm (1 ft) high. Sterile and fertile fronds are distinct, the former being glabrous, pinnatifid and spreading, while the fertile fronds stand erect and have entire pinnae.

  W. virginica, N. America, grows 45–60 cm ($1\frac{1}{2}$–2 ft) high and is similar to preceding except for the fertile fronds, which are narrowly divided. Evergreen.

Grasses and reeds

ARUNDO *(Graminae)* giant reed
Stout reedy stems with—in warm climates only—large plume-like panicles of flowers. Arundos need plenty of sun and moisture but should not be exposed to cold drying winds.

  A. donax from southern Europe grows to 3 m (10 ft), or larger in warm countries, with stout leafy stems of glaucous, long narrow leaves. Although superior, the cream and green variegated 'Versicolor' or 'Variegata' is not as hardy as the type.

BAMBOOS
Background plants with grace and elegance which are not only useful as wind-

breaks but set off smaller plants most pleasingly. None do it better than the giant grasses known as bamboos. Their airy habit causes them to bend and sway with each breath of wind, the leaves rustling and whispering in the breeze like village gossips. All delight in deep, rich, loamy soil, especially where they have an annual mulch of well-rotted manure and leaves to retain soil moisture. Plant them in spring and provide plenty of water the first season. Propagation is normally by spring division, and since some kinds can be rampant it is important to keep them under control by removing surplus stems from time to time. There are no hardy *Bambusa* species, although they can be grown in frost free countries. In colder climates their place can be taken by species of *Arundinaria*, *Phyllostachys*, *Shibataea*, *Sasa* and *Chusquea*.

CAREX *(Cyperaceae)* sedge

A large genus of grassy perennials with triangular stems, a few suitable for the bog garden. In Kent the leaves of some species were at one time used to tie up hops; in Italy they are employed for caulking barrels and weaving grass covers for wine flasks, and in Lapland sedges are used to stuff gloves and shoes as a protection against cold. Propagation by division.

Recommended are C. *pendula*, Europe, including Britain, bright green leaves and brownish spikelets; C. *pseudocyperus* which has drooping, many-flowered spikelets of green which look something like slender catkins; C. *riparia*, the greater pond sedge of the northern hemisphere, best represented by the heavily white-striped 'Variegata', which grows to 60 cm (2 ft) and has brown spikes of flowers in summer; and C. *stricta* 'Bowles Golden', which was found in the Norfolk Broads and grows about 38 cm (15 in) high with brilliant golden leaves.

COIX *(Graminae)* Job's tears

C. *lacryma-jobi*, a grass from tropical Asia which produces large, pearly-white to lead-coloured seeds from rather insignificant flowers. It is suitable only for frost-free climates or may be grown as an annual for indoor pools. The seeds are often fashioned into necklaces, especially in China.

CYPERUS *(see* p. 57)

ERIOPHORUM *(see* p. 60)

GLYCERIA *(see* p. 61)

JUNCUS *(see* p. 63)

MISCANTHUS *(Graminae)*

Tall perennial grasses of robust growth allied to *Saccharum*, the sugar cane, and often listed as *Eulalia*. All appreciate a moist sunny position with deep rich soil; the crowns of the variegated kinds benefit from a mulch of dry leaves in winter as they are less hardy than the type species. Propagated by division.

M. sacchariflorus (*Imperata sacchariflora*), Japan. Commonly known as the hardy sugar cane, this vigorous grass grows to 2.7 m (9 ft) with long arching leaves which rustle in the breeze and are retained in the dry state all winter. It is often planted to form a protective hedge or screen, although it only flowers in warm climates, producing terminal panicles of silvery-mauve spikelets.

M. sinensis, China and Japan. A robust grass reaching 1.5–2.4 m (5–8 ft) in height. The grey-green leaves are striped with white and have suffusions of grey in 'Variegatus'. 'Silver Feather' produces arching sprays of pinkish-brown leaves, and 'Zebrinus' has golden bands across the foliage.

PHALARIS *(Graminae)* ribbon grass
P. arundinacea 'Picta' (gardener's garters), northern hemisphere. A handsome grass with flat blades longitudinally striped with white, and biscuit coloured flowers in late summer and autumn. Invasive. Propagated by division.

PHRAGMITES *(Graminae)*
P. communis, the well-known Norfolk reed, used for thatching but of cosmopolitan distribution. A strong, rampant reed suitable only for lakeside plantings or wildlife cover, growing 1.8–3 m (6–10 ft) high with broad leaves and heavy plumes of purplish flowers.

SCIRPUS *(Cyperaceae)* bulrush
A large and widely distributed genus found in wet moors, bogs and marshes. Few are worth growing in gardens, being much too invasive.

S. tabernaemontani 'Albescens', with round pithy stems of 1.5–1.8 m (5–6 ft), green with white vertical stripes, and the zebra rush, *S.t.* 'Zebrinus', 30–90 cm (1–3 ft), which has its stems transversely banded in green and white—like porcupine quills—are both worthwhile plants for wet mud or shallow water. Propagated by division.

SPARTINA *(Graminae)* cord grass
S. pectinata (*S. michauxiana*), N. America. A tough, invasive grass sometimes used to bind banks, but only garden-worthy in the clone 'Aureomarginata', a 120 cm (4 ft) plant with ribbon-like leaves which droop at the tips and are striped with yellow; green flowers in autumn. Propagated by division.

ZIZANIA *(Graminae)*
Z. aquatica (Canadian wild rice, water oats), N. America. An annual grass growing 2.4–2.7 m (8–9 ft) high with broad flat leaves, reedy stems and large, terminal panicles of flowers; to 30 cm (1 ft). Often planted for waterfowl and in some parts as food for humans. Raised from seed.

12

Troubles in the water garden

Cloudy water

Discoloured water looking like pea soup is the cause of most complaints from pond owners. It defeats the whole purpose of having a pool if one cannot see the fish, it looks unpleasant and constant emptying and refilling with fresh water only gives a temporary respite.

When water turns green it is due to the presence of myriads of unicellular plants called algae. These may be conveyed on plants or animals or borne on the wind but once they alight on the pool they feed on dissolved mineral salts in the water, and if there is a fair amount of light, thrive and multiply. It follows that the richer the salts and the more open the position the more the algae increase. Incidentally, green water is not harmful and even provides food for fish fry but it looks so unsightly that most people ignore its virtues.

Usually the original trouble lies in the compost. It is essential that loam used for planting aquatics is fibre-free and when bonemeal or cow manure is added it must not be in direct contact with the water but covered with plain loam or shingle (see p. 22). Similarly organic manures like horse dung, rabbit and poultry manures, as well as leafsoil and peat are best avoided. They contain too much fibre or humus and during their breakdown release organic gases and salts to the water, altering its chemical content and encouraging algae. The smaller the pool the quicker the balance can be upset.

REMEDIAL MEASURES
Use only recommended composts and keep down their organic content. Introduce plenty of oxygenators; water is never discoloured in pools or lakes which have a good carpet of underwater vegetation. The best kinds for rapid results are elodeas, lagarosiphons, callitriches and myriophyllums. Shield new pools from strong sunlight naturally with water lily foliage and tall aquatics on the sunny sides. Brown cloudy water is usually caused by such fish as tench and carp, which remain on the floor of the pool and forever root into and stir up

mud. Green or brown floating scum can be removed by either flooding over the pool or driving it to one corner with a hose, then drawing a newspaper across the surface. This picks it up.

Remove fallen leaves and any dead weeds as these will cause de-oxygenation whilst rotting down, charging the water with chemical salts and adversely affecting the fish. Today there are biological filters which work on a similar principle to the older type sewage farms. These have to be of a size approximately 10 per cent of the water surface and should be placed out of sight away from the pool. They are operated by a small pump which takes the water from the pool and spreads it evenly over porous filter media where bacteria digest any impurities. The water is then returned to the pool by means of gravity. You can obtain up-to-date information on this comparatively new development from your aquatic specialist. I have tested this method, which resulted in crystal clear water!

Blanketweed

A collective name for several types of filamentous algae which form hair-like tresses that twirl around both submerged and emergent plants.

Proceed as suggested for discoloured water by limiting the provision of food and light by the introduction of plenty of submerged oxygenators, which also afford shade. Remove long strands of blanketweed with a notched stick, twisting this round and round in the material so that it adheres and can be pulled out, or else use a rake for the same purpose. Avoid chemical controls if possible. Most of these can be dangerous and alter the chemical nature of the water.

Aphids

The water lily blackfly (*Rhopalosiphum nymphaeae*) can be a great nuisance, particularly in warm summers, when it breeds at a prodigious rate and completely covers water lily leaves, buds and stems, also frogbits, sagittarias, flowering rushes and other aquatics. Spray the pests forcibly with a strong jet of water. This knocks them into the water where they will be taken by fish. Repeat as necessary. Alternatively, force all floating leaves and flowers under water for 24 hours, holding them down with a hoop of wire or a weighted sack. Cut back to water level any aquatics which cannot be submerged.

Caddis flies and mosquitoes

The caddis fly larva uses pieces of aquatic plants to make pupa cases, thus spoiling the plants, which they also eat, and mosquitoes are a source of irritation to humans. In both cases fish such as goldfish and golden orfe will deal with these pests.

Brown china marks moth

These small moths with brown scribbly markings on white wings appear in summer, laying their eggs in clusters on water lily leaves. The larva cuts out pieces of foliage, sticking them on the undersides of the leaves. When these are opened green or black caterpillars can be found inside. Since they change homes several times this disfigures many leaves. Handpick the caterpillars in small infestations or forcibly submerge the foliage as suggested for aphids.

Water lily beetle (Galerucella nymphaea)

Both larvae and adults of this beetle, which is dull brown and about the size of a ladybird, feed on water lily leaves and flowers. Eventually these become a sodden mass of dark decaying tissue. Spray forcibly to dislodge the pests so that fish can devour them or submerge the foliage as recommended for aphids.

Water lily leaf spot

Two leaf spots affect water lilies, both resulting in disintegration of the foliage. A *Cercosporae* sp. causes the leaf edges to become dry and crumble while *Ovularia nymphaerum* produces white spots which spread rapidly, after which the leaves rot in patches. Remove and burn infested leaves.

Snails

The freshwater whelk, *Limnaea stagnalis*, is the worst of the freshwater snails which attack water plants and in particular will rapidly destroy submerged oxygenators. It increases rapidly, laying its eggs in jelly-like masses on the undersides of water lily leaves. Handpick to remove or place a cabbage or lettuce stump in the water. Remove this daily and shake off the adhering snails.

Herons

These usually visit ponds very early in the morning to take fish. They are difficult to deter but if wire is stretched just under the surface a little way in from the sides, it often stops them from walking into the pond. Herons do not fly on to the water but go in from the edges. An artificial heron poised near the edge has also proved effective in some instances (see p. 21). Small ponds may be netted over.

Frogs, newts and cats

In spring frogs, newts and toads come to water to breed, but rarely do any harm. Moreover the adults are the gardener's friends and get rid of many pests, so leave them alone. Their visit is purely temporary. Cats sometimes hook fish out of pools for the hell of it. A well-aimed missile is the best deterrent. They soon learn.

13

Livestock in the pond

Even when gardeners do not deliberately introduce livestock to a pond, sooner or later the water teems with a rich variety of life. Many of these creatures are invisible to the naked eye but others—flying to the pool or carried as eggs or larvae on plants, or adhering to the feet and fur of birds and visiting animals— may develop to snails, beetles, and similar easily discernible water animals.

All these have their part to play in the balanced community of the pond life. From the gardener's point of view, however, some may not be welcome, for there are creatures which prey on plants and spoil the look of ornamental aquatics; while dragonfly and beetle larvae, together with certain types of fish, are so pugilistic that they jeopardize the lives of others.

Fish

Although fish are not essential to the maintenance of still water, yet the advantages of introducing them are so great that most people will wish to include them. These benefits may be summarized as follows:

(a) They are aesthetically pleasing and bring a 'live' interest to the pond. In no other form of gardening is there such a visible relationship between plants and animals.
(b) Still water encourages mosquitoes, which breed freely during the summer months. Fish destroy the larvae and so are helpful to man.
(c) Many pests of water plants—aphids, water-lily beetles, and the like—are consumed in the egg or larval stage by fish.
(d) They 'fertilize' the pond plants with their excreta and provide carbon dioxide (exhaled in breathing) for use by submerged oxygenators in photosynthesis. Further details of this process are given on p. 76.

In the ornamental garden, only bright and easily seen fish, which normally live near the surface of the water, make desirable pond inmates. Certain species, such as tench and mirror carp, find their food in the soft mud at the bottom and so keep the water in a constant state of muddy agitation. Not only is it then impossible to see them, but they so foul the water that everything else in its depths becomes obscured. For this reason there seems little point in introducing carp, rudd, and tench to ornamental waters, especially when more suitable varieties are available.

There are also fish which are inimical to other species. Catfish and stickle-backs, for instance, are so pugnacious that docile, slower-moving types become fair game and are harried unmercifully. Wounds made with their spines frequently turn septic, so that goldfish especially often die, leaving the bullies in sole possession. It is also unwise to put small specimens of the same breed in a pond with very large ones, unless there is plenty of submerged vegetation in which the former can hide. It is the practice of fish to devour their own progeny, so an abundance of oxygenators are necessary if any youngsters are to survive.

Shade is necessary for fish and is normally provided in a mature pond by the floating leaves of lilies and neighbouring aquatic vegetation. With a small pond in an exposed position, a few overhanging rocks at the pool edge or some hollowed-out stones placed in the water, so that fish may rest beneath them, prove effective in breaking the force of the sun's rays.

Fish should not be introduced to a new pond until it has been matured and the plants are growing freely. In the case of a concrete pool this may take several weeks, but with pond liners and prefabricated pools the fish may normally go in two or three days after planting. It is also unwise to net new stock on arrival and transfer them in this manner to the pond. Handling of any kind is undesir-able as the eyes particularly are easily damaged (fish have no eyelids) or the scales may be rubbed from their sides. These injuries may prove fatal and also allow disease to develop which can spread throughout the community. The ideal method is to lower the can or the plastic bag in which they have arrived into the pond and let them remain like this, until the water in bag and pond are at approximately the same temperature; then tip the container on its side and let the fish swim out.

The best fish for ornamental pools are goldfish and their varieties, minnows, and golden orfe. Streams and lakes can of course accommodate larger and coarser fish—such as rudd, tench and in some cases trout, although these tend to remain low in the water so may not often be visible. Never introduce pike however unless you want all the other fish to disappear. These are the sharks of fresh water with voracious appetites. In warm climates or with indoor pools and aquaria the choice is very much wider; there are many tropical species so a visit to a good specialist establishment will be worthwhile, if you contemplate having fish in these conditions.

The common goldfish (*Carassius auratus*) is native to the Orient and varies in colour from pearl, silver, and black to rich gold, sometimes with patches of several shades on the one fish. Eggs are laid in early summer, and although the fry on hatching are all dark in colour they gradually lighten so that most adult fish become red or red and black in two or three years.

There are many varieties, some grotesque, others very beautiful, mostly developed by the Japanese and Chinese. They may have long and flowing tail and fin developments like the fantails and veiltails, elongated bodies such as the comet, or strange wart-like excrescences on their heads like the orandas and lionheads. Others show unusual body colouration, as the velvety black moor, which can also have a drooping tail like a veiltail; or the shubunkin, which is often known as the calico fish because of the mottled shades of black, gold, red, blue, mauve, and cream which can all be found on the one individual. The more blue and mauve (a rare colour for goldfish) the better the fish.

There are also strange forms with protruding eyes—the telescopes, which can be further distorted by a perpetual squint upwards in the celestials. Most of these more grotesque forms need a certain amount of care and attention and will not long survive in the outdoor pond. They are also expensive and in every way more fitted to the indoor pool. Comets and shubunkins, however, are perfectly hardy and can live outside with ordinary goldfish in temperate climates.

But undoubtedly the most colourful fish among the hardy kinds are Japanese koi and hi-goi carp. They are also the most aristocratic. Unlike shubunkins, which have few visible scales, the scales of koi carp are very pronounced and come in various brilliant metallic colours—basically bright gold or silver spangled with combinations of red, black, silver and blue in bold striations. They also grow very large, up to 2 kg ($4\frac{1}{2}$ lb) each, and are easily tamed to feed from the hand. They have large appetites, requiring protein food like small worms, tubifex, daphnia (waterfleas), rubbed raw meat as well as pelleted food obtainable from dealers. Being naturally bottom feeders however they tend to stir up mud in the pool and root into water plants so are really only suitable for a large pond. They also like well oxygenated water and appreciate fountains and waterfalls. But they are very expensive to buy so it might be wise to start with something less ambitious if you are a new pond owner.

The golden orfe (*Idus idus* var. *orfus*) is extremely hardy and lives happily with goldfish. Its slender, pencil-shaped body is well adapted to quick movement and, as it usually swims in shoals, is easily discernible darting across the surface of the water. Golden orfe often reach 30–38 cm (12–15 in) in length in captivity but rarely breed in Britain.

The minnow (*Phoxinus phoxinus*) is a small fish (rarely exceeding 10 cm (4 in)) sometimes caught in the wild and added to the pond. It is a harmless species and extremely useful in keeping down mosquito larvae and other pests.

Other natural fish, such as green tench, roach, rudd, etc, are useful in large or deep shady pools to destroy mosquitoes, but since they stir up the mud they should not be introduced into small or ornamental ponds. Dace like running water, sticklebacks are quarrelsome and must be kept by themselves, and mirror carp, king carp, common carp, and golden carp all grow to a large size but prefer to keep to the bottom of the water, so are rarely seen.

Japanese hi-goi carp are the most colourful among the hardy kinds of fish.

FEEDING

Many fish in large ornamental stretches of water frequently survive with no artificial feeding at all, for most ponds contain a certain amount of such natural food as mosquito larvae, water fleas (daphnia), fly and beetle larvae, snail eggs, and the like. In small artificial pools, however, supplementary diet is necessary for growth and survival.

But this must not be overdone. Two or three times a week in summer enough food should be provided to be entirely consumed in five minutes. Nothing at all need be given between November and March.

Winter is the natural resting period of fish. Respiration is markedly decreased as is their assimilative ability so that little or no food is required during this quiescent period. *But they must be well fortified before the fast*, so good feeding is essential in autumn. From September until the first week in November foods rich in protein—such as rubbed raw meat, dried daphnia, Bemax, pulverized hard-boiled egg, chopped earthworms, and the like should be given several times a week. These foods can be alternated with one of the well-balanced, proprietary brands of biscuit meal, although only sufficient of these should be given at any one meal for the fish to consume in five minutes. Any left after this time falls to the bottom of the pond, where it is out of reach and soon starts to rot.

Early in November the fish turn sluggish and artificial feeding should cease entirely until spring (March). Sometimes a bright winter's day induces them to swim near the surface, but do not be tempted to feed on that account. They will survive on stray water creatures and the layer of autumn-accumulated fat in their bodies. Digestive troubles—which account for many spring deaths—often follow indiscriminate winter feeding.

A similar good protein diet is necessary in spring to recover stamina and build up body strength; resistance to disease is low at this time owing to the long period of fasting, and many fish fall victim to illness if not looked after.

Fish appreciate variety in diet and any of the following can be interspersed with one of the proprietary brands of prepared dried fish food: flaked boiled fish, Bemax, pulverized hard-boiled egg, rubbed raw meat, chopped earthworms, bloodworms (larvae of the *Chironomus* fly), minced liver, or flies.

Always feed in the same place, and the fish will come to associate you with the provision of food and in course of time even take titbits from your hands.

Other livestock

While a naturalist welcomes and even encourages all kinds of water creatures to the pond-side, snails are not essential, but will probably reach your pond anyway, carried by birds or on plants. It is true that they are scavengers and clear up much debris but too many of the wrong kinds can constitute a nuisance. The best kinds are those which normally do not include plants in their diet, notably the ramshorn snail (*Planorbis corneus*), with a shell shaped like a Catherine wheel, together with its red-fleshy variety *rubra* and the freshwater winkle (*Paludina vivipara*). The freshwater whelk (*Limnaea stagnalis*) and other limnaea species are less selective in their diet and show a lamentable liking for the choicer floaters and submerged aquatics.

All snails are hermaphrodite and so breed fast, but fish destroy many of the eggs, which helps to keep them in check. Limnaea can also be trapped by laying a cabbage or lettuce stump in the pond overnight. They flock to this and can be removed with the bait the following day.

Frogs, toads, and newts visit ponds in spring and lay their eggs in gelatinous masses. Although this annoys many people (and it must be admitted that the eggs disfigure the water for the time being), these useful creatures do so much good in trapping insects the rest of the year that I hope most gardeners will tolerate their presence during the breeding season. The adults soon leave the water and the tadpoles follow directly the legs appear and they are able to fend for themselves. Thereafter they become the gardener's friends and consume many of the enemies of his plants.

Index

Index